Facebook Mentoring and Early Childhood Teachers

This volume explores concepts of mentoring, leadership and issues faced by early childhood teachers. Foregrounded against inadequate leadership and mentoring training in this sector, this book looks at how mentoring is exercised through Facebook. Mentoring through Facebook provokes a strong sense of freedom in terms of speech and influence. The benefits for using social media in mentoring includes minimising costs and reaching mass numbers of mentees globally where knowledge can be shared and information gained. Whilst there is also a positive and active approach to mentoring, there is the danger of mentoring that misinforms, disempowers and alienates.

This book will help active players in the early childhood sector in understanding the crucial nature of mentoring and its impact when used through Facebook and similar social media sites.

Sharryn Clarke is a lecturer at Monash University in the education faculty and has a background in early childhood education. She has previously worked in a variety of settings including teaching and operating education and care services, an education advisor in early intervention and as an assistant manager at the Victorian Department of Education and Training. She currently teaches a variety of units relating to policy development, partnerships, leadership and professional studies as well as child development and learning. Sharryn's research areas include mentoring and social media, family engagement and environmental studies.

Routledge Research in Early Childhood Education

This series provides a platform for researchers to present their latest research and discuss key issues in Early Childhood Education.

Books in the series include:

An Interdisciplinary Approach to Early Childhood Education and Care
Perspectives from Australia
Susanne Garvis and Matthew Manning

Challenging the School Readiness Agenda in Early Childhood Education
Miriam B. Tager

Narratives in Early Childhood Education
Communication, Sense Making and Lived Experience
Edited by Susanne Garvis and Niklas Pramling

Animals in Early Childhood Education
Diahann Gallard

Dance-Play and Drawing as Semiotic Tools for Young Children's Learning
Jan Deans and Susan Wright

Facebook Mentoring and Early Childhood Teachers
The Controversy in Virtual Professional Identity
Sharryn Clarke

For more information about this series, please visit: www.routledge.com/Routledge-Research-in-Early-Childhood-Education/book-series/RRECE

Facebook Mentoring and Early Childhood Teachers

The Controversy in Virtual Professional Identity

Sharryn Clarke

Routledge
Taylor & Francis Group
LONDON AND NEW YORK

First published 2018
by Routledge
2 Park Square, Milton Park, Abingdon, Oxon OX14 4RN

and by Routledge
711 Third Avenue, New York, NY 10017

Routledge is an imprint of the Taylor & Francis Group, an informa business

British Library Cataloguing-in-Publication Data
A catalogue record for this book is available from the British Library

Library of Congress Cataloging-in-Publication Data
A catalog record for this book has been requested

ISBN: 978-1-138-68142-2 (hbk)
ISBN: 978-1-315-54585-1 (ebk)

Typeset in Times New Roman
by Apex CoVantage, LLC

This book is dedicated to my teenage daughters, Milly and Eva, who taught me that Facebook isn't for everybody and who taught each other not to believe everything you read on Facebook. Thank you, my wise souls.

Contents

Preface

> We simply cannot afford to ignore the issues [for children] if we want to succeed in a world where what is needed are competent, intelligent and socially capable people.
>
> (Stanley, Richardson, and Prior 2005, in Council of Australian Governments 2009, p. 6)

This monograph presents research findings that are part of a larger study, which investigated current mentoring practices through Facebook and sought to determine what beginning early childhood teachers believe to be fundamental influences upon their growth and professional identity as well as early childhood pedagogical values entering the workforce. Facebook has become a household name for persons of all walks of life. Many institutions use this medium to promote and connect their core business with a targeted audience. However, sometimes these promotions and connections do not always result in positive outcomes, in particular those Facebook sites that aim to lead our future generation of teachers. With the significant change in the Australian early childhood sector through national reforms, as well as a lack of quality training in leadership and mentoring, new teachers turn to Facebook for guidance and networking. Social networking provides the ability for educators to develop connections, learn from each other and discuss pedagogical constructs. This includes opportunities for informal, or as some referred to as 'ad-hoc' mentoring between early childhood experienced teachers and beginning teachers. A significant gap of research exists regarding the effects of mentoring through Facebook on Australian early childhood beginning teachers as they begin to develop their professional identity.

The first phase of the larger study, as outlined in this monograph, analyses the perceptions, discussions and arguments emerging between mentors and beginning teachers on a number of Facebook sites specifically focused upon early childhood practices. To explore the concepts of identity and self-efficacy the philosophy of Martin Heidegger has been used as a theoretical framework. This approach discusses the sense of 'being' in terms of the beginning teachers as they transition from student, to teacher and as part of being a teacher, 'the mentee teacher.' This theory has also been used in the same manner regarding experienced teachers who offer an ad-hoc mentorship through Facebook sites. Using a phenomenological approach as the methodology, data were collected in an unstructured manner from participants on the Facebook sites.

Emerging themes in the findings included members calling out for advice, whilst other times they would like to challenge a philosophical approach to learning and teaching. Additionally, they also used the Facebook site as a general request to just 'have a rant.' Further findings that emerged through some sites was that many of the experienced teachers' posts who were acting as mentors to beginning teachers were also seeking mentoring from others on the same Facebook site posing a potential concern that inexperienced and untrained 'mentors' are advising the 'mentees.' The themes represented three streams of engagement and content, namely 'hot topics,' 'sharing,' and 'emotionally driven expressions.' Each stream describes the type of engagement as well as the nature of responses from members, which may include helpful mentoring, conflicting mentoring or condescending mentoring, and how this may impact upon the perceptions, thoughts, feelings of efficacy and actions of the beginning teacher in their teaching practice.

Acknowledgements

The development of this book has stemmed from the conversations and debates with many people who have had a significant impact upon my way of seeing the world, including social media. Firstly, I would like to acknowledge and sincerely thank Professor Sivaneswary Phillipson who has been by my side throughout this research project and given me the confidence and courage to keep thinking, keep exploring, keep understanding and keep writing! Your guidance and mentorship means the world to me and has ignited a passion for research.

Secondly, I would also like to thank Professor Susie Garvis for her guidance and support in exploring what everyone might or might not be really saying on Facebook and how sometimes literal contexts are not literal at all, and at other times they might be. Your wisdom has opened my eyes to so many possibilities.

Thirdly, I would like to thank Dr Hanan Sukkar who inspired me to write with caution when exploring such controversial topics to make sure the reader was not swayed by my own dogma, but could see an unfolding picture that they could make sense of themselves. Your honesty and authenticity has helped me to keep it real.

To my patient and understanding family who have had to stay quiet or go out so that I could write and understand when I needed to be 'in a moment' to keep the writing flowing. Your love, support and encouragement have kept me going throughout this research project and those times of distraction to watch cats get up to crazy mischief was sometimes my saving grace. Chris, Milly and Eva, I thank you.

Finally, I would like to acknowledge the early childhood sector for their visible presence on social media and dedication to the profession. Your discussions, guidance and support to each other sees a force that can take the profession to further levels of wisdom and enlightenment which will ultimately impact upon those we serve – children.

Abbreviations

ACECQA	Australian Children's Education and Care Quality Authority
DEECD	Department of Education and Early Childhood Development (Victoria) (former)
DET	Department of Education and Training (Victoria) (current)
DETE	Department of Education, Training & Employment (Queensland)
DoE	Department of Education (Federal)
ECA	Early Childhood Australia
FB	Facebook
NQF	National Quality Framework
NQS	National Quality Standard
PLP	Professional Learning Program
SNS	Social Networking Sites

Glossary of terms

Blog A website that publishes and displays posts from one or multiple users, generally detailing events, opinions and ideas in chronological order.

Blogger A person who writes and maintains a blog.

Metadata Data that is created by users conducting online tasks or communicating electronically with others. Specifically, this is the registered action that has occurred (e.g. phone call, date of post, etc.), however not the actual content of what has been typed or said.

Post A statement or paragraph of text that is published on an online forum using an SNS such as Facebook.

Poster A person or member of an online forum that creates and publishes a post on an online forum.

1 Introduction

1.1 What this monograph is about

The purpose of this monograph is to enlighten the reader firstly of the existence of typical conversations that occur on Facebook between beginning and experienced early childhood teachers, and secondly how these conversations impact upon the reader and members within the actual conversation. As it is an interpretive analysis, it is taken from a bird's eye view that ponders the meaning behind the posts, comments and conversations of the Facebook members. It sets up a foundation of inquiry into the rationale behind the nature of engagement in social media, in particular the nature of ad-hoc mentoring as it is seen on 'screen' and not with face-to-face personal engagement with the members. To understand the in-depth themes and nature of discussion that occurred on Facebook, it was firstly essential to establish the concepts behind the purpose of inquiry, which is highlighted below. What follows is an exploration of literature that discusses mentoring and the impact this can have upon beginning teachers as well as aligning mentoring with the phenomenon of social media and its significant rise in utilisation by humanity, including implications of its usage such as Facebook addiction and legal ramifications. Furthermore, the findings within this monograph aim to raise further questions to stimulate and enable additional exploration and therefore investigate in real-time, with real early childhood teachers, both beginning and experienced their personal encounters with Facebook mentoring. It describes the beginning of what now seems to be a much larger scope of study than once anticipated. This monograph is the foundation of inquiry that forms this initial piece of curiosity; what are early childhood teachers actually saying on Facebook and why might they be saying it?

As an avid user of Facebook myself, both for personal and professional reasons, I have come to realise that social media seems to be having a profound impact upon humanity, including myself. Initially I was drawn to and surprised by the negative impulses or trolling that were occurring on general sites and relative cyber bullying that captivated a wide audience. It also occurred to me that there might be as much positivity on Facebook as there were questionable and somewhat dogmatic interactions at times. However, in the beginning of this process of inquiry I was not completely sure. I wondered if this general obsession with checking Facebook posts also existed within professional networks such as educators in early childhood, in particular new teaching graduates otherwise known as *beginning teachers*. Whilst Facebook has the tendency of changing socialisation as we know it (as you will read further) I wanted to know if it really was having an impact on beginning teachers in the real world, and if it was, what sort of impact? Were beginning teachers giving up on teaching altogether because of the confronting and possibly self-promoting mentoring on Facebook, at the expense of the beginning teacher? Or were they savvy enough in their selection of mentoring and resilient in how they received and used their advice in their everyday practice? I felt that this was important to know as this interaction lies within our professional obligations as mentors, teachers and supports ourselves. If we, as a collective group of mentor teachers are to ensure consistent improvement in the teaching world, we firstly must be reflective upon our own practice. This also includes how mentors engage in their online conversations such as the interactions on Facebook as what could once be very private mentoring is now very public, even in a 'closed (private) group.' It is not necessarily one beginning teacher that can be affected, but many. Therefore, the scope of impact from the mentor is now not confined to the mentor–mentee relationship; it has broadened to a point where one mentor may impact thousands of mentees at the posting of a single comment or the click of the 'like' button. The importance of this research reaches beyond the beginning teacher. In fact, the most vulnerable recipients of the impact are children. This very reason was the significant motivator in discovering the impact Facebook mentoring is having upon the decisions beginning teachers make when they are teaching young children. However, before I could explore these questions, I needed to establish how Facebook was used by early childhood teachers, both beginning (mentees) and experienced (mentors), the conversations that were had and how they were conducted, which is exactly what is explored in this monograph.

1.2 The new way of *being* together

Communication as we now know it has taken a significant leap forward and somewhat sideways in the context of social media and its continuous influence on society in general. No longer do we have to sit patiently for the long-awaited letter in the post; instead as a society we have instant communication with each other through social network sites (SNS). The urgency of this form of connection becomes forthright in our lives through the immediate ease of access on our smartphones, our tablets, laptops, desktop computers and now with the introduction of the iWatch, our body. We have Wifi hotspots in shopping centres, fast food chains, on public transport and even on flights. We can be contacted at any time, in any place, by anyone.

According to van Dijck (2013), social media has recently risen to high levels of popularity and in the last 10 years the interactive culture of today, including socialisation is conducted online more than ever before. Ferris and Wilder (2013) define *social media* as an electronic web-based platform that acts as an enabler for users to connect with communities through online interaction. Boyd and Ellison (2007) further define the term *social networking site* (SNS) as a service that is exclusively web-based and allows members to not only create public profiles, but to also list connected members in relation to their interests and preferences as well as explore and engage with connections made by others. In saying this, the participation is not determined by lists and connections alone, but by the encounters experienced through these connections and the data one provides on their profile page. Networking in this manner provides opportunities for connections to be made with both friends and strangers who have similar interests or mutual friends/connections. Data is collected through the sites that can link people together in terms of their likes, interests and groups they belong to. This is the genius of Facebook that was founded by Mark Zuckerberg in 2004 when he was attending Harvard University (Good, 2012; Ross et al., 2009). From small and local beginnings, it rapidly grew to be a global phenomenon that is not only a part of the daily lives of humans, it is shaping how we communicate, connect and live as humans. Facebook is now one of the most widely used social networking sites estimating "845 million active users, 50% of whom log onto FB at least once a day" (Hall, Pennington, & Lueders, 2014, p. 959).

Alongside the rise in the use and connectivity of Facebook, there has been a significant shift in early childhood education in Australia through a number of national reforms, both legislative and pedagogical. These reforms have changed the nation's agenda in relation to the needs within the early childhood sector, in particular change in perceptions, teaching approaches and a focus upon learning outcomes. Australian early childhood educators now also find themselves with additional roles and responsibilities such as mentoring and leadership; however, they have not been equipped to perform these roles due to lack of training (Stamopoulos, 2012). Furthermore, there seems to be a reluctance in experienced early childhood practitioners to take on formal mentoring roles due to unfamiliarity with newly introduced theoretical frameworks or philosophies, lack of confidence, heavy workloads and once again inadequate training in leadership and mentoring (Campbell-Evans, Stamopoulos, & Maloney, 2014; Walkington, 2005).

Concerns exist for both the early childhood graduate (who will be known as the *beginning teacher*) as well as the children in their care. Early childhood practitioners have a profound effect on children's learning and development despite the fact their pre-service training may not have influenced quality practices in their daily work with children (Cummins, 2004). The experiences pre-service teachers have had during their degree often influences their professional disposition along with their personal belief systems and teaching styles which can further lead to a variety of practices that may seem inappropriate (Cummins, 2004; Giovacco-Johnson, 2011). Macfarlane and Noble (2005) agree that initial teaching experiences of pre-service teachers strongly influence the teacher's beginning and ongoing effectiveness as a teacher once they graduate. It is therefore clear that the manner in which beginning teachers are originally trained and then mentored in the field can not only determine outcomes for their future capabilities and skills as a teacher, but also the learning and developmental outcomes of the children they teach.

The new reforms have caused a pedagogical discourse in the experienced early childhood field as veteran teachers try to make sense of and implement new early childhood frameworks and legislation, and perhaps feel challenged by the pedagogical shift in the sector (Ortlipp, Arthur, & Woodrow, 2011). Nailon (2013) further implies that organisational control and the push for similar educational perspectives and values can dominate the thinking of teachers. As a result, learning environments for pre-service teachers and beginning teachers can be confusing and strained, with pedagogical reflection, challenges and arguments creating awkward workplaces and relationships (Nolan & Sim, 2011). Furthermore, educators in early childhood are often uncomfortable in their role as a leader perhaps due to lack of effective training and therefore beginning teachers' experiences both in pre-service training and in graduate years may impact negatively (Campbell-Evans et al., 2014; Fenech, 2013).

So what happens when the rise in the use of Facebook coincides with the lack of effective leadership and mentoring for early childhood beginning teachers? To explore how this connects, it is important to firstly consider the concept of mentoring and leadership and what is happening right now on Facebook and other social media sites. According to Rothwell and Chee (2013), mentoring and leadership can go hand in hand and that some mentors can be considered leaders. Both elements of influencing people (leadership) and inspiring and encouraging behaviours (mentoring) can be combined. Rothwell and Chee further believe there are also different ways to be a mentor that incorporate strong elements of leadership such as leading by example, storytelling, teaching directly or reflection of our own experiences. However, as the early childhood sector is traditionally noted for lacking in adequate leadership, consultation and expert knowledge (Stamopoulos, 2012) mentoring has become somewhat of an ad-hoc system partially due to a lack of investment in early childhood leadership and mentoring training (Fenech, 2013; Walkington, 2005). In the push for future leadership and mentoring in early childhood, we run the risk of finding the sector flooded with self-proclaimed mentors and consultants basing their advice on personal dogma, rather than empirical evidence and research. In fact, Dunn, Harrison, and Coombe (2008) claim that the early childhood field prefers conferences and curriculum references rather than engaging in research to validate their professional stance. This preference can also create strained relationships between supervision teachers (potential mentors) who undervalue research and pre-service and beginning early childhood teachers who have experienced research as part of their pre-service training (Dunn et al., 2008).

Whilst it is difficult to find literature evidencing the phenomenon of the influx of consultants mentoring graduates without empirical evidence for their guidance, it only takes a number of views on consultants' website blogs and social media sites to see strongly formed opinions and unsolicited advice being served to others. For example, one blog site known as *Anarchy and the EYLF Pirates* whose motto declares 'Refuse. Resist. Rebuild.' challenges the Early Years Learning Framework (EYLF) concept regarding agency stating "All approved frameworks require the provision of agency however an unambiguous understanding of agency does not exist, isn't routinely evident in day to day practice" (Anarchy and the EYLF Pirates, 2015, para. 2). In another blog of the same author titled "Can you rate 'quality' objectively?" (Anarchy and the EYLF Pirates, 2014), the newly introduced Assessment and Rating Process in Australia is considerably questioned as to its reliability in being able to assess quality, claiming that the process has political influences and subjective ethical boards to approve such processes. Consultancy *Inspired EC* used its blog site to challenge teachers at times of festivities, reminding them to consider their philosophies before they act by stating

> What bothers me though is that in our attempts to fully embrace the festive spirit, many services and educators appear to abandon their philosophies and subsequently, children's rights. Services who usually wouldn't allow a stencil to make it's (sic) way in the front gate all of a sudden have Christmas crafts were [sic] every child makes an identical footprint reindeer.
>
> (Inspired EC, 2014, para. 2)

Semann and Slattery, a consultancy and research organisation based in Australia, also blog to support educators in their wellbeing and often (but not always) utilise peer-reviewed literature to illustrate their point. For example, in their blog, Director Anthony Semann addresses professional behaviour on Facebook stating "I value the fact that others don't think like me, but I just don't get why people take offence when their colleagues choose to think differently and consequently go on a verbal rampage online" (Semann, 2015, para. 4).

This leads to questions about the methodology beginning teachers use to make decisions regarding the effectiveness and appropriateness in the mentoring they receive through social media as some organisations promote the mentor (or experienced other) as always knowing better, potentially oppressing the mentee and their innovation (Hargreaves & Fullan, 2000). From these examples, there are both positive and negative aspects of blogs bearing in mind that well-regarded mentors can be highly influential, not only to beginning teachers, but also to experienced teachers who also may be mentoring others. Dunn et al. (2008) implies there is much work to be done to deploy new and inspiring leaders and mentors to maintain momentum in "attaining continuous renewal of the profession" (p. 703) in quality early childhood education. Further to this, the importance of advice and mentoring that is strongly based upon ethical and rigorous research must be incorporated to validate and provide some empirical evidence for the advice.

Importantly, beginning teachers may bring with them new teaching pedagogy that may be unfamiliar to experienced mentors and even consultants, yet equally useful or applicable (Hargreaves & Fullan, 2000). Depending upon personality types and leadership styles, experienced mentors may find this challenging. The National Reforms, as previously mentioned, instigated a strong pedagogical shift in response to receiving poor results in international reports (Fenech, 2013). This has resulted in the development of new national and state policies that doctrine what is to be done in education and care settings. This includes the National Learning Framework, better known as *Belonging, Being and Becoming; The Early Years Learning Framework for Australia* (EYLF) and in Victoria, the *Victorian Early Years Learning and Development Framework* (VEYLDF). Both frameworks have strikingly similar pedagogical approaches that are strongly based upon more contemporary theories such as sociocultural theory, post-structuralist theories and cultural-historical theories. Of less significance, or at least challenged in relevance to current-day practices are the once-heralded Cognitive Development Theory of Jean Piaget or Erikson's psychosocial theory that formed strong foundations for Developmentally Appropriate Practice (DAP) ensuring that programs are engaging and responsive to children's development (Copple & Bredekamp, 2008). The paradigms focussing upon child development as sequential such as these are challenged by academics such as Fleer (2005) who stated "that the term 'child development' as used within the field of early childhood education in Australia is found wanting" (p. 6). Fleer challenges the relevance of DAP despite it being a core element of pre-service training for many years in Australia and thus still in the United States of America. Instead, Fleer claims that the development of children must also be seen through the lens of their culture and societal paradigms rather than 'typical' sequential stages and refers to theorists such as Rogoff and Vygotsky to support this shifting focus of theory (Fleer, 2005). This shift has supported beginning teachers in developing their teaching styles in line with the sociocultural and cultural-historical theories as well as post-structuralist theories relating to philosophers such as Foucault and Deleuze. As pre-service teachers experiencing their undergraduate programs, their exposure to these contemporary theories are more detailed and weaved through a number of practical elements of their training.

Whitehead and Krieg (2013), in their comparative study of two pre-service teachers spanning almost 100 years, detail the significant changes in pre-service early childhood teacher training that has also made an impact upon the pedagogical approaches in the sector itself. The case studies specifically focus upon a student in the early 1900s, and end with the perspectives of a recent graduate. From the first case study where Froebel and Dewey were studied closely with a strong link to psychological studies as well as teaching approaches such as the Montessori Method, we see a significant change in focus with a strong emphasis on learning and post-structuralist theories highlighting the inclusion of co-constructing learning between teachers and children (Whitehead & Krieg, 2013). This is where graduates currently sit as they are taken on a journey of the 'regimes of truth' from the likes of Michel Foucault and question gender under the provocations of Judith Butler. In light of this, we also see more significantly the shift from behaviourism and the influences of Erikson and Skinner, to the Vygotskian approach where learning is led in complexity but not dictated (Whitehead & Krieg, 2013). Whilst re-known theorists such as Jean Piaget and Jerome Bruner remain within context of teacher training, there is a stronger focus upon more abstract and creative ideologies such as Rogoff's sociocultural theory utilising three foci of analysis in terms of assessing learning and Gardner's multiple intelligence theory in terms of exploring learning dispositions. Situated alongside the change in this theoretical shift, there has also been the significant inclusion of incorporating the ideology that learning begins at birth and not merely at ages 3 and 4. Cheeseman, Sumsion, and Press (2014) articulate this very concept by stating "The introduction of state endorsed curricula documents for children from birth is consistent with the view that preparation of future citizens begins well before compulsory schooling and that there is benefit for government to invest in such a measure for very young children" (p. 408). Meanwhile experienced teachers have had to seek this knowledge independently, and perhaps unwillingly as they may already have a strong sense of who they are and which professional practices they maintain (Ortlipp et al., 2011).

Furthermore, experienced teachers may not have professional mentoring training themselves in learning and applying to their practice such complex contemporary ideologies. The clash of professional practices and pedagogy through mentoring runs the risk of oppression in the beginning teacher, should the experienced mentor adopt an approach that contradicts what the beginning teacher has learnt in their degree and in turn makes them feel incompetent in their knowledge and skill (Stamopoulos, 2012). In contrast, we may also see the mentee teacher reject the traditional values and pedagogy of DAP that were once held strongly in Australian education culture and linked with Piagetian theory (Aldwinckle, 2001). This creates a problematic situation both for the mentee and mentor if they struggle to share their pedagogical beliefs and understandings and apply them in their teaching.

Research regarding leadership in early childhood is limited, and there appears to be more study in this field regarding school systems (Fenech, 2013). The research that does exist seems to come from a select few authors and focusses upon types of leadership models that can be utilised in early childhood settings such as distributive leadership (Fenech, 2013). Despite this, there still is the argument that inadequate leadership research in relation to the thoughts and opinions directly received from early childhood practitioners is still prominent (Stamopoulos, 2012) and are more international, rather than in an Australian context (Ortlipp et al., 2011). In addition, Ortlipp et al. (2011) demonstrate concern in the lack of studies accomplished in an Australian context regarding the professional identity of early childhood practitioners, whilst Desimone et al. (2014) states that there is also sparse research or comparative studies of the effects of informal and formal mentoring for the same teacher. We see that many leaders in our sector have not had specified leadership training and cannot articulate effective leadership strategies to support beginning teachers (Campbell-Evans et al., 2014). Of further concern is the minimal emphasis of research in feedback variables which plays an enormous role in the effectiveness of mentoring and can contribute to protégé anxiety attachment (Allen, Shockley, & Poteat, 2010). Mentees with protégé anxiety attachment may be less receptive to feedback due to feelings of insecurity and a reluctance to hear anything negative about their performance (Allen et al., 2010).

Whilst research regarding mentoring in early childhood is limited, there are some articles that identify the importance of the relationship between the mentor and the student teacher during early childhood practicum placements in pre-service training (Loizou, 2011). A variety of emerging factors to consider in this relationship is the impact the mentor has on the beginning teacher, particularly in relation to personal theories and pedagogy, and learning and developmental stages (Loizou, 2011). To begin the exploration of how mentors might be impacting upon beginning teachers through engagement on Facebook, it is firstly important to understand and define mentoring.

1.3 Mentoring

The definition of mentoring

The concept of mentoring dates back to Greek mythology when Odysseus (in Latin, known as Ulysses) employed an Ithacan noble and trusted friend, named *Mentor*, as guardian to his son Telemachus whilst he was away during the Trojan War. Mentor's role was to guide, teach, protect and counsel Telemachus in Odysseus's absence (Nosheen Rachel, 2013; Sanfey, Hollands, & Gantt, 2013) therefore emerging the concept that a mentor is a trusted guide and teacher, filled with wisdom, support and sound advice (Rothwell & Chee, 2013).

Mentoring is defined as matching more experienced role-models with a novice or new personnel, with the idea that the wisdom and expertise they have gained from experience and teachings can be passed to their less-experienced protégé (Colomo-Palacios, Casado-Lumbreras, Soto-Acosta, & Misra, 2012). It is expected that the mentor will develop an atmosphere of trust with their mentee to help them overcome obstacles in their working life, build competence and self-esteem and stronger capabilities within themselves (Koç, 2012). A mentor is seen as a leader to the protégé, both by example and in reflective practice.

The purpose of mentoring

In recent times, researchers have taken considerable efforts to explore the impact and effects of mentoring on future professionals across a range of vocations. Colomo-Palacios et al. (2012) suggest that publications on mentoring in the fields of education and social sciences have significantly increased over the last two decades, indicating that the practice is now receiving far more attention as a tool for building best practice than ever before. Mentoring is now widely used across schools, business organisations and government agencies, aiming to improve quality practice and productivity, and retention of teachers (Hallam, Chou, Hite, & Hite, 2012;

Rothwell & Chee, 2013; Stamopoulos, 2012). Whilst there are many claims that mentoring provides benefits to performance improvement, perhaps firstly what is important is to understand the act of mentoring through exploring various types of mentoring.

Types of mentoring

In terms of mentoring in early childhood, leadership is seen as a shared responsibility across professionals as they collegially work through changes in educational and pedagogical approaches (Stamopoulos, 2012). Furthermore, there are various forms of mentoring such as formal mentoring and informal mentoring with the latter demonstrably more valuable as they are more natural, spontaneous and positive, including much knowledge sharing (Colomo-Palacios et al., 2012). I will now describe the differences between formal and informal mentoring to outline the links to mentoring practices in social media.

Formal mentoring

Similar to many professions, teaching also includes both formal and informal mentoring practices; however formal practices tend to be more prevalent in primary and secondary education in Australia, and less frequent in the early childhood sector, although in 2016, the Effective Mentoring Program (www.vit.vic.edu.au/registered-teacher/how-to-train-as-a-teacher-mentor) has been extended to early childhood teachers as they are now required to undergo formal teacher registration as also required by their primary colleagues. This program is funded and co-ordinated in partnership between the Victorian Department of Education and Training (DET) and the Victorian Institute of Teaching (VIT) aiming to support beginning teachers in their standards of teaching progressing through to full registration by training mentor teachers in effective mentoring (DET, 2017). Prior attempts had been made to formalise mentoring in early childhood settings through the Education and Care Services National Quality Standard (NQS) in terms of ensuring that each education and care service has adequate access to an educational leader (ACECQA, 2013) who could be deemed as the service's mentor. The NQS defines the Educational Leader as "the person the approved provider of an education and care service designates in writing to be a suitably qualified and experienced educator, co-ordinator or other individual to lead the development and implementation of educational programs in the service" (p. 197). In this context, the Educational Leader acts both as a formal mentor and facilitator of educational programs. The effectiveness of this in terms of driving progress and successfully enabling and uplifting mentees is yet to be determined.

Prior to the Effective Mentoring Program, Victoria had also taken some steps to pilot some structured mentoring programs for early childhood educators as mentioned previously. One such pilot program indicated positive results in formal mentoring as mentees gained enriching experience through the mentoring relationships. The findings, however concluded that more work needed to be done in relation to mentoring in early childhood, in particular with isolated teachers (McCartin, Nolan & Beahan, 2014). This mentoring program at that stage, nevertheless, did not differentiate for beginning teachers.

Earlier studies identify that a systematic approach to mentoring should be taken and include strategic planning such as goals of the program, functions and preparation of the mentor and how mentors and mentees should be matched (Poldre, 1994). Poldre further discusses that evaluating the mentoring programs should be integral in the systematic approach to mentoring. A systematic approach embedded within the framework has the potential to achieve this.

Informal mentoring

Informal mentoring also plays a crucial role in the development of professional practice and according to Sanfey et al. (2013) can advance a mentee's career prospects and remuneration rather than those receiving formal mentoring alone. They further claim that there is a personal element to informal mentoring as mentors act as role-models and support mentees in understanding and combining both personal and professional responsibilities (Sanfey et al., 2013). Mentees who have formal and informal mentors are less likely to leave the profession as they develop further learning and skill in their teaching (Desimone et al., 2014). In further analysis of the differences between formal and informal mentoring, Desimone et al. iterate that whilst formal mentoring designates a more evaluative role, informal mentoring could actually be more productive due to its absence of accountability.

Often informal mentoring occurs when beginning teachers choose those they consider to be expert in their profession and they willingly seek help and guidance from these experts (Desimone et al., 2014). In this context, there is no formal or robust analysis or evaluation of the mentoring relationship and the professional or unprofessional practice resulting from this. Informal mentoring can occur within or outside the mentees' organisation, and in fact is open to a large array of sources, including social media. Often there is no formal structure or systematic way to provide the mentoring and therefore is potentially not evaluated for best practice or intentions. More importantly, evidence suggests that it is the informal mentoring that has a significant impact upon the future teachers yet educational policy and mentoring initiatives are yet to catch up with this phenomenon. As stated by Coburn (as cited in Desimone et al., 2014, p. 88) "informal networks among teachers are largely unacknowledged by the policy world. Yet they have enormous potential to play an influential role in teacher sense-making." When it comes to social media, it becomes evident that informal mentoring serves a strong place in teacher development, particularly beginning teachers.

The benefits of mentoring

Researchers specialising in the study of mentoring have determined that employees who are mentored have more job satisfaction, commitment and career progression as well as higher remuneration (Baranik, Roling, & Eby, 2010). This is also the case in the teaching profession as Koç (2012) states that effective mentorship strongly contributes to professional growth in student teachers, as well as retaining teachers in the workforce (Desimone et al., 2014; Stamopoulos, 2012).

Benefits of mentoring teachers has a lineal effect where research has identified that mentoring can also improve student achievement as teachers become more knowledgeable and confident in their identity (Desimone et al., 2014). Positive effects and teacher progress is particularly noticeable when mentors are appropriately matched in areas the novice teacher is struggling in, such as mathematics (Desimone et al., 2014). Rothwell and Chee (2013) claim that benefits are also reciprocal as the mentor also finds reward and pride in seeing their mentee grow and develop, gains respect from others and builds a support network of current and past mentees.

What is effective mentoring?

To make these gains and benefits through mentoring, one must consider what is effective mentoring as not all mentoring experiences result in positive outcomes. According to Cummins (2004), effective mentoring includes mentors who are open to self-improvement, model their reflexivity and share their expert knowledge with the mentee. Mentoring does not have a sense of supervision or accountability, but relational trust and honesty that encourages reciprocal learning and growth (Cummins). Mentoring is more effective when organisations have carefully chosen whom they permit to be a mentor, to ensure that mentoring practices do not have a negative impact upon the mentee (Baranik et al., 2010). Further to this, negative experiences of mentoring can in fact reflect the core values of the organisation as a whole (Baranik et al., 2010). In context of early childhood, one could suggest that negative mentoring on beginning teachers might then reflect poorly upon the early childhood sector as a whole.

Effective mentoring is more likely to be gained if mentees have mentors that are located within the same school (Desimone et al., 2014), or in the case of the early childhood sector, organisation or service. This provides better logistics to meet regularly, to get to know each other better and develop a systematic approach to mentoring activities. People who are involved in mentoring within their organisation are less likely to leave their employment (Rothwell & Chee, 2013). Koç (2012) further claims that the duration of mentoring can also impact upon the effectiveness and professional outcomes of mentees. Eller, Lev, and Feurer (2014) state in their studies of mentoring novice nurses that effective mentoring relied upon maintaining open communication and accessibility, passion and inspiration, exchange of knowledge, mutual respect and trust and caring, personal relationships.

What makes a good mentor?

In seeking effective and positive results of mentoring, particular characteristics, skills and personalities must be considered in what actually makes a good mentor. The way a teacher feels about their mentor can have an impact upon their relationship including their perception of the mentor, frequency of interactions and nature of discussions (Desimone et al., 2014). Good mentors will also have been provided with specific mentoring training to improve their quality in mentorship (Koç, 2012) and ensure longevity in the relationship. Research has identified particular qualities that should be included in the skill set of a good mentor such as ensuring they have available time to remain in frequent contact with their mentee and gain a professional rapport and closeness, as this tends to have more positive results with the mentee's outcomes (Hurd & Zimmerman, 2014). The personality of a good mentee is also crucial with traits of open-ness and acceptance rather than being judgemental or threatening (Dunham-Taylor, Lynn, Moore, McDaniel, & Walker, 2008). Being an enabler is considered by Rothwell and Chee (2013) to be a vital quality in a good mentor, as well as being an engaging storyteller to illustrate their relevant experience. Good mentors are willing and ready to go the extra mile for their mentee, will recognise that they may not be suited or experienced enough for a particular mentee, will create a safe learning environment and role-model reflective practice (Rothwell & Chee, 2013). A good mentor will also "encourage and demonstrate confidence in a mentee, ensure a supportive environment and provide frequent feedback" (Sanfey et al., 2013, p. 716).

The mentors and mentoring in this research

In deciding upon the criteria of what constituted a *mentor* in the context of this research, the definition as previously described appeared to evolve and expand according to perceptions of those who considered themselves a *mentor* to *someone*. Dunham-Taylor et al. (2008) describes mentoring and the relationship between the mentor and the mentee as "a form of planned socialisation, with the mentor as the socialising agent" (p. 339). Furthermore, Sanfey et al. (2013) describe the mentor as someone who is more senior in their role and experienced in their profession, earning respect from the newly graduated and less experienced. They further refer to mentees as somewhat of a 'protégé,' who is nurtured in their professional growth by the mentor to bring them to success and achievement. Sanfey et al. (2013) also state "qualities of a successful relationship include honesty, active listening, flexibility, reciprocity, mutual respect, a personal connection, and shared values" (p. 715), which illustrates the importance of these personality attributes in the mentor. In this sense, the term *mentoring* has a distinct hierarchal relationship with the *all-knowing* and the *less-knowing*, however is flexible enough to acknowledge new information and conceptual ideas that might be brought to the relationship from either party. In terms of the Australian early childhood context in the current climate, this definition however does not always seem applicable, particularly in light of the change in legislation and lack of sector knowledge in the pedagogical and legislative shifts of the sector, as well as lack of leadership, especially in a formal sense. Recalling that leadership training is minimal in Australia and that often formal mentors are difficult to find, the definition of mentoring as it currently exists today must be further explored.

The Facebook pages investigated were specifically selected due to the membership context and its relevance to this particular study. Upon analysis of members, all pages included a vast array of experienced and inexperienced as well as degree qualified, diploma qualified and unqualified members. Membership included a clear mixture of professional backgrounds and employment or educational settings, as well as professional roles of those using social media as a means of professional and personal development and seeking and/or giving advice. The selection observed included the following:

- Beginning teachers, such as graduate teachers, as mentees,
- Educators employed and also studying for their degree who considered themselves 'mentees,'
- Degree and master's students studying full-time and not employed with some considering themselves 'mentors' whilst others 'mentees,'
- Teachers who had returned to work after a period of absence, either due to maternity leave, personal choice or study and considered themselves 'mentees,'
- Teachers who had been working in the field between 2–6 years and considered themselves 'mentees,'

- Teachers who had been working in the field between 5–30 years and considered themselves 'mentors,' and
- Non-practicing teachers and tertiary employees who had experience in the field but were now working as consultants to the sector and considered themselves 'mentors.'
- Early childhood leaders and managers working in local or state government or other non-government organisations acting as mentors.

In context of this research, the definition of 'mentor' can therefore include a professional teacher (Diploma or Bachelor trained) who has been working in the field either part-time or full-time for at least 4 years. This of course does not imply that the 'mentor,' according to this definition, contains the skills, knowledge and attitudes required for effective mentoring as previously stated. This then potentially becomes a dilemma.

The search for specific pages devoted to supporting Victorian beginning teachers alone also proved to be difficult as it became apparent that the same members used a variety of pages also, including nationwide early childhood education pages and others devoted to specific jurisdictions such as New South Wales. Likewise, some members on specifically dedicated Victorian pages were actually living and working in other states or territories. It was difficult to limit the analysis of the Facebook pages to Victoria alone and therefore the analysis included members from various states and territories of Australia. Given that education and care services are governed by a national legislation, this approach continued to be deemed appropriate and relevant to the content.

The mentees – early childhood beginning teachers

One of the first experiences of mentoring an early childhood beginning teacher has is in their pre-service training. There has been recent research regarding the professional placements that student teachers undertake and the importance of the development of professional identity. Pre-service teachers feel they are not prepared for the workforce upon graduation with one of the major concerns being their preparedness and confidence in their ability to manage behaviours that are challenging (Galman, 2009; O'Neill & Stephenson, 2012). Pedagogical influences from supervising teachers can have a strong effect on the pre-service teacher's understanding of course materials, which in turn further determines their ongoing practices as beginning teachers (Fajet, Bello, Leftwich, Mesler, & Shaver, 2005). Pedagogical influences and efficacy were particular features of Ortlipp and Nuttall's (2011) study regarding the impact supervising teachers have upon pre-service early childhood teachers where English is not their first language. Their study indicated that supervising teachers had to interpret course material for pre-service teachers to assist them in making sense of it, despite having no support or guidance from the tertiary institute themselves to do this (Ortlipp & Nuttall, 2011).

Garvis (2011) provides a recent example of the influence of supervising teachers in her study of the inclusion of arts in early childhood programs. She indicates that supervising teachers play an integral role in influencing pre-service teachers on their placement through modelling their practices, and persuading the pre-service teacher to see and do things from their perspective (Garvis, 2011). Another issue concerning pre-service teachers is the level of mental conflict or dissonance in their practice and ability intruded upon them by experienced others either in professional placement or training programs. Whilst a healthy level of dissonance can support the pre-service teacher to reflect upon their practices, higher levels can create conformity and lack of agency and confidence as they graduate and continue their journey as a teacher (Galman, 2009). In contrast, some supervisory teachers minimise the amount of conflict to ensure pre-service teachers have a happy placement, however this runs the risk of encouraging a lack of self-reflection (Galman, 2009). O'Neill and Stephenson (2012) claim that beginning teachers are also more likely to maintain their employment if they develop a good sense of confidence in their ability and knowledge. When this is challenged, or if they don't feel this sense of efficacy, beginning teachers tend to become stressed and burnout quickly. This is particularly evident for early childhood beginning teachers in their second year of teaching (Macfarlane & Noble, 2005). In their study, Macfarlane and Noble illustrate that early childhood teachers may have a romanticised view of their profession whilst they are in training which can be exacerbated by course materials and practical placement. However once in the field, the romantic view suddenly shifts as reality sets in (Macfarlane and Noble, 2005), raising the risk of beginning teachers starting to doubt their ability and suitability to the field.

Further impacting upon pre-service teacher's professional identity is the current industrial conditions in Australia for early childhood educators working in long day care, which are notably long hours with low pay and little professional recognition. Boyd (2012) reports that studies conducted with early childhood graduates in Australia indicated that only 6% intended to work in child care, leaving a very large gap in our workforce. Having strength in their professional identity can reduce the high amount of early childhood beginning teachers leaving the sector (Stamopoulos, 2012).

Macfarlane and Noble (2005) suggest that beginning teachers are more likely to develop positive skills and attitudes in developing their pedagogical stance if they are supported by strong professional networks. This can support how they think and act and reflect upon experiences they have had in their pre-service training (Giovacco-Johnson, 2011). The process of emerging from pre-service teacher to beginning teacher to experienced teacher is therefore a journey of the development of professional identity. Cartmel, Macfarlane, and Noble (2004) suggest that critical reflection is vital and can be achieved through learning circles consisting of experienced practitioners and pre-service or beginning teachers to provide safe opportunities to confront their thinking, acquire multiple perspectives and develop new understandings of their work with children, impacting upon their practice.

A further way to continue this reflexive development is through professional mentoring as it can foster two functions: one being psychosocial whilst the other is developing careers of the mentee including professional identity (Eller et al., 2014). Unfortunately, effective mentoring programs specifically designed for early childhood pre-service teachers as they graduate have previously been few and far between, leaving a gap in the sector and potentially risking higher levels of attrition. Mentoring programs that have existed include the following:

- *Professional Mentoring Program for Early Childhood Teachers*, conducted in partnership with Deakin University, Victoria University and the DEECD (now DET) (McCartin et al., 2014).
- *The Coaching Program*, co-ordinated by a partnership between Gowrie Victoria and DEECD (now DET), evaluated by Dr. Delwyn Goodrick.
- *Early Childhood Education Workforce Capacity Project*, An Introduction to Mentoring for Early Childhood Educators, conducted in partnership with Western TAFE NSW, Batchelor Institute of Indigenous Tertiary Education, Riverina TAFE NSW and Charles Sturt University (Coombe, 2011).
- *Mentoring Program for Indigenous Early Childhood Educators*, under the *Indigenous Professional Development Project*, Queensland, funded by the Australian Government and managed by the Queensland Department of Education, Training and Employment (DETE).
- *Professional Support Coordinator*, in every state and territory, funded by the Australian Government and in partnership with a variety of agencies through tender. In Victoria, this is Gowrie Victoria.
- *Educational Leadership in Early Childhood Settings* and *Leading People*, under the auspice of Bastow Institute of Educational Leadership, funded by DET (formerly DEECD) and tendered by private organisations such as Semann and Slattery Pty Ltd.

Whilst this is not an exhaustive list, it is limited to a small proportion of early childhood educators and not necessarily pre-service or beginning teachers. As a result and in an attempt to seek support and advice from experienced others, beginning early childhood teachers have often turned to social media. However, perhaps it is in this space that the lines cross as to who is actually the mentee and who declares themselves to be the mentor?

1.4 Social media, Facebook and our changing sense of being

The phenomenon of social media

The concept of social media has existed from as early as 1997 through a site known as *Sixdegrees* (Kietzmann, Hermkens, McCarthy, & Silvestre, 2011). This particular site enabled members to develop profiles as well as add friends to their list of contacts and even friends-of-friends to continually broaden their networking boundaries and send each other messages. In 2000 *Sixdegrees* closed due to financial constraints with possible reasoning that it was ahead of its time and therefore did not correlate with the then usage of the internet which was still emerging in some industries (Boyd & Ellison, 2007). Over the years various SNSs began to emerge and the concept of networking began to infiltrate through more than just dating sites and friend's circles, but more complex communities such as LunarStorm, Ryze.com, Friendster and eventually in 2005 on the public arena, Facebook (FB) (Boyd and Ellison, 2007). Features that were exclusive to Facebook that has made this site a phenomenon itself included the addition of applications available to allow the member to create more personalisation to their profiles such as creating timeline journals and travel features, sharing statuses and uploading photographs, video and files (Boyd & Ellison, 2007; Hall et al., 2014). Facebook also acts as a form of journaling where members can archive photographs, special events and holidays, as well as notifications of birthdays (Kaun & Stiernstedt, 2014). Facebook can enlighten, empower as well as deflate depending upon the nature and timing of posts, which also includes a number of activist pages addressing political, global and social issues. Kaun and Stiernstedt (2014), in their exploration of the temporal aspects of experiences on Facebook, also suggest that previous research implies Facebook can and has also included elements of self-care. This is notably seen as posts and re-posts of inspirational quotes attached to aesthetically attractive photos and illustrations, health advice and scientific articles as well as invitations to support groups for various social and health concerns. This then brings us to the exploration of the variety of Facebook sites that are available for the purposes of life-long learning and how we integrate this with our daily lives, including teaching practices and pedagogy. In essence, there is a Facebook page available for everyone.

The human engagement with social media has now changed our professional networking methods and has evolved the human condition in the way we socialise and engage with others in leisure activities (Jordan, 2013; Vanwynsberghe & Verdegem, 2013). Vanwynsberghe and Verdegem suggest that as humans, we no longer find only ourselves in life-long regimented friendship groups classified by identity, but we can also associate with a larger variety of groups across global communities, possibly exploring and changing our identity. They also warn that one must consider the terms regarding how social media is used as the concept of private versus public information is blurred. This controversial concept maintains high profile in current political trends as the Australian Federal Government enacts its legislation on the collection and retention of metadata. The Attorney-General of the Australian Government stipulates that metadata is only stored for 2 years and is for the sole purpose of the safety of Australian citizens and any contact that had been made from those suspected of criminal activity such as terrorism, assault and kidnappings ("Telecommunications (Interception and Access) Amendment (Data Retention) Act 2015," 2015). However, alongside the introduction of this legislation are claims of 'invasion of privacy' of the Australian people. For example, journalist Harry Tucker for news.com.au writes "This scheme is allegedly being implemented to protect the country against organised crime and terrorism, but it is also being slammed as a major invasion of privacy" (Tucker, 2015, para. 2). ABC news reporter, Will Ockenden also challenged the nature in which the government collects metadata through the use of tracking mobile phone devices (Ockenden, 2015). As social media becomes a part of daily life, so too does the tracking of government agencies on our communication habits. In saying this, the purpose of using social media to network, mentor and connect teachers together appears to largely deviate from criminal activity, yet potentially be at risk of civil law cases of defamation or libel due to the published nature of social media.

In exploring the very nature of early childhood professional discussions on social media there is potential for the conceptual understanding of educational constructs to be blurred or misguided depending upon the context in which it is used and re-used or re-posted on social media sites. Comments from social media users imply their own interpretation of the information, which can then influence others in their perspective or even information receipt of the original post. Jordan (2013) further highlights that communication is not restricted to dedicated social media sites alone, but broadens to the recreational habits of internet users, including gaming and online servers. He suggests that identities can also be blurred in the form of an avatar or code-name and that users are left to analyse by the nature of communication as to the possible presence of their networking connections. An avatar is a fictional alternate identity, icon or character that is chosen by the user to protect their true identity including any links to their life outside of the virtual world. They are often used in video games, particularly online gaming and on internet forums. This brings us back to the example of the blogsite Anarchy and the EYLF Pirates where avatars or fictional identities were used instead of the true identity of the blogger who could also potentially be a high-profile early childhood mentor, or someone without any early childhood training or knowledge at all. We therefore question, who are we when we are on social media sites?

Who are we really? Heidegger's challenge to our virtual identity

Identity, whether it be professional, personal, real or virtual plays a significant role in the lives of humans. Chryssochoou (2003) argues that identity has transformed from a rigid exemplification of behavioural and scientific variables that attempts to explain motivation and action, to now being a social representation of *self*. She further states that identity incorporates the way we see ourselves as well as the way we see our 'self within our world' or multiple words which implies that we may have multiple identities according to the particular world we see ourselves in at the time – virtual or real. This includes what our identity looks like to others also as a symbolic entity or real appearance. Of particular importance is that "knowledge about oneself is fundamentally social in the sense that it constitutes a particular form of social thinking concerning the self" (p. 227). This means that in order to present our identity to others, we must firstly understand what our identity is in context of the world to which we bring that particular identity. Highlighting the essence of identity and ways this can be connected to the mysteries and phenomena surrounding social media is the philosophy of Martin Heidegger.

Heidegger was a notable German philosopher and scholar who originally studied theology but abandoned this to explore further the concept of logic (Wisnewski, 2013). Heidegger's mentor Edmund Husserl was the founding father of phenomenology and as Heidegger used and explored this research approach, he also extended it to further reaches of understanding including multiple perspectives of classical philosophies such as those of Aristotle. His most distinguished manuscript *Being and Time* was considered the work of a genius as it intricately examined the concept of Being which in this research closely relates to the discussion of identity in terms of who we are online and offline (Polt, 2005; Wisnewski, 2013). Heidegger proposed that as humans, we must understand the difference between *Being* and *Beings* which also distinguishes the difference between the physiological self and the philosophical self; our existence of mind in time and place. Therefore, we might think more figuratively rather than literally as we explore this concept. The use of Heidegger's philosophical understanding of Being in this study features two significant aspects; it explores and challenges identity and our *sense of being* as well as brings to the forefront the use of phenomenology in this exploration. The constructs arising from this philosophy that are examined include destabilisation, intentionality and de-situation which highlights the existential nature of this study where the participants are instrumental in determining their own existence through free acts of will. All three terms were not necessarily coined by Heidegger himself, but have evolved through an interpretivist approach to understanding his philosophy and applying the essential components to this study.

Destabilising the identity

In his essay "Why Reawaken the Question of Being" Grondin (2005) argues that humanity's obsession with the concept of existence – who we are, our Being – is a journey for *truth of self* (Grondin, 2005). In saying this, Grondin argues that Heideggerian theory further proposes that one also flees from knowing this truth as questioning our very existence is *destabilising;* that is, it destabilises what we know of our Being. This term implies that our understanding of our Being is not certain as we have not questioned who we are, but have instead continued to avoid this line of questioning as the answer may bring about uncertainties that may be too disquieting to face. We therefore flee from our actual Being to create an alternate existence or multiple existences, ones which we can define the boundaries for and have particular controls around. Our destabilised Being can be likened to the avatars, code-names and pseudonyms used in social media networking sites where only the virtual Being of ourselves is present and our real self has possibly fled in that particular time and space. Despite this, our virtual self may still have elements of our real self in order to produce in the first place, the identity we want others to see. By doing this, our full Being may potentially become destabilised as we question the truth of our real existence and not just our virtual Being. In relation to Facebook mentoring, we must consider that whilst mentors are happy to give advice and provoke the sector in their thinking, it may not always be authenticated in the acknowledgement of their actual Being and identity to others and therefore one questions, 'do they stand behind their name and their voice whilst they are using social media?' Would they argue the same points in person as they do online? Further anomalies may exist around multiple virtual Beings raising destabilisation to a further level of complexity. Is it possible that the mentor parading as one virtual Being may also be another virtual Being with opposing viewpoints? In understanding how Facebook is constructed, it is possible that one's virtual Being presents differently across multiple sites, therefore destabilising even the virtual Being. This concept of *destabilisation* raises the issue of the mentor's credibility in their mentoring as whilst they offer their expertise, their certainty in their opinion is questionable as they flee from judgement or challenge from others of their real self simply by only using their virtual identity or as Grondin (2005) states, "an inauthentic form of existence" (loc. 410).

If we combine the aforementioned attributes of effective mentoring and what makes a good mentor with Heidegger's concept of Being, we begin to ask ourselves the authenticity of mentoring that currently exists through social media, despite many are still drawn to it as their form of enlightenment and advice, even in career progression. Furthermore, applying our concept of Being to a 'virtual' world leaves room for creativity in terms of 'designing one's *self*' according to how they want to be seen, rather than who they really are. Hall et al. (2014) claims that the information contained in the personal profile can both provide opportunity for self-promotion, whilst also experiencing challenges should the member not be able to match the public profile in reality. "For the actor, SNS provide ample opportunities to fashion desirable and even misleading impressions" (p. 959). This is where the concept of ego may align itself with the member's emotional connection to Facebook and how their public image is represented and responded to. Hall et al. (2014) further explore and discuss the connections between the real self and the online or virtual self through the use of warranting theory, which determines the artefacts posted by the member to warrant authenticity of the member's profile or deem the member hypocritical or mistrusted. They suggest that when online users create misleading profiles, they make it difficult for their connections to know and believe what is true and what is not, according to what they do, say and think. This also could be the case with mentoring using social media as some early childhood mentors may potentially over-promote their abilities and practices perhaps leaving an impression upon mentees that is different to the reality in their teaching practices. This leads to the second construct arising from the interpretation of Heidegger's theory, known as *intentionality*.

The intentionality of mentors

As we have seen in the explanation of destabilisation, the identity of mentors as presented on social media sites can be lined with inauthenticity as a means to protect the actual identity of the poster. However, it is the intention of one's actions in creating or designing this virtual identity that is the underlying concern here. Why is it that they do this? *Intentionality* is something that Heidegger explored regarding the subjective perception and thoughts in one's mind and the authority to reveal these thoughts according to their level of self-awareness (Crowell, 2013). It is important to understand however that the concept of intentionality was not designed nor originated by Heidegger, nor by his mentor Edmund Husserl. It was in fact originated by Husserl's teacher Franz Brentano, an Austrian philosopher, psychologist and priest who considered that intentionality provided a means of understanding objects separate from the physical Being, but more from the mental understanding – the intention of mind (Crowell, 2013). In other words, something exists because our mind intentionally sees the object for what it is and decodes and understands the use of the object according to our intentional interpretation. Husserl extended upon this to include 'acts' and how these are perceived through relative consciousness, however Heidegger avoids this term and instead uses 'care' bringing a more subjective and practical element to the nature of intentionality, as Crowell describes Heidegger's perception that "the possession of intentional content requires a further condition: I must be able to understand myself as *being* up to something at which might succeed or fail" (p. 25). This brings us to the relativity of this study, whereby intentionality is seen through the lens of Heidegger's understanding of Being.

Bringing us back to the question of *Why is it that they do this?* (as in design or create a virtual identity on Facebook), we may consider that the destabilisation of one's identity may actually be intentional and a result of a subjective perception that one has regarding their skills and abilities as a mentor. This means that the mentor acts as a mentor on Facebook because they see themselves as a mentor, regardless of whether they have the actual skills and attributes of a mentor. It is their intention therefore to be *seen* as a mentor by others. Their actual Being may not come into question, particularly if they are using an avatar or fictional identity, as they have intentionally chosen not to disclose this or reveal who they really are. Crowell (2013) further argues that Heidegger questions this concept of self-awareness (or self unawareness) in the very confronting use of the term 'I' particularly through the lens of the first-person, focussing upon the practices of a person, rather than only what goes on in one's head. For example, a mentor who sees himself or herself as a mentor does so by practice and the typical actions of a mentor, rather than merely thinking *I am a mentor*. The intentionality of this is to 'act as a mentor' but not necessarily 'be a mentor.' This 'act' can be also viewed in terms of the 'third-person.' The concept that 'I am a mentor' is only apparent if others *see me as a mentor*. The *intention* then shifts from the first-person to the third-person where it is the third-person who determines whether the mentor actually is a mentor (be it act or not) and therefore the mentor's Being is subject to the intentional perception of the mentee (see Figure 1.1).

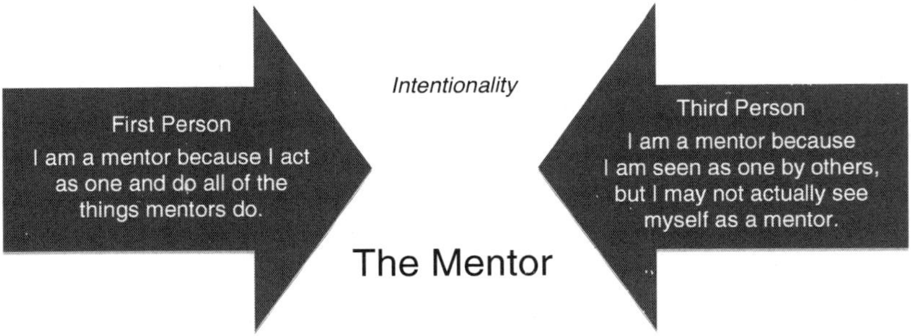

Figure 1.1 Exploring Heidegger's concept of Intentionality in relation to The Mentor

In terms of this study, and according to the juxtaposition of the first- and third-person, according to Heidegger the term 'I' can appear as two different conceptual Beings in that the mentee can also be the mentor and vice versa depending upon the intention of the interaction. Defining oneself as a mentor in its purely subjective term could mean that a new graduate could see themselves as a mentor if they portray themselves to be so. Alternatively, an experienced teacher could portray themselves as a mentee and inadvertently be mentored by a graduate. The destabilisation of identity through social media allows for this, particularly if there are some levels of anonymity attached. Intentionality therefore creates the platform for destabilisation and in turn brings about ambiguity of Being in relation to mentees and mentors. The view of authentic mentorship and effective mentoring is brought to the forefront of the argument with the vital piece of the puzzle remaining within the intention of the mentor and their purpose for being a mentor or being seen as a mentor. In addition, we question this intention and the existing understanding and professional training that mentors or mentees may or may not have regarding good and effective mentoring and how they might use this. As mentioned before, intentionality is apparent if the mentor is *seen as a mentor* but in order to be seen in this way, the mentee also has to have an understanding of what a mentor actually is. We ask again, who are we when we are on social media?

The de-situation of mentors and mentees

MENTOR OR MENTEE: THE INDISTINCT IMAGE

Now that social media can play a part in our social identity of that we wish to or do not wish to disclose and the plight of the shifting pedagogical and industrial sands of the early childhood sector, there are possibilities that mentors are mentees and mentees could very well be mentors. This exchanging of roles relates to the educative backgrounds of both experienced teachers and beginning teachers including their pre-service experience, relevant content of university teachings and the manner in which the sector is positioning both. Aside from this, there is a very strong societal shift in how we view ourselves, our acquisition of knowledge, the usefulness of this knowledge that we have and the manner in which we share it.

The obsession with Facebook and our ever increasing need to share our news, ideas and opinions has now somewhat become a conundrum in recognising who we actually are and our intention of who we want to be seen as. Vishwanath (2014) addresses this phenomenon stating that the obsession with checking Facebook profiles has resulted in "therapists and counselors (sic) reporting an increase in the number of Facebook 'addicts' speak(ing) to a sort of compulsivity in the use of Facebook" (p. 83). What we can see here is that society has shifted dramatically to a need for continued and seamless social engagement with those not presently in the room, but presently and accessibly in the virtual world. Vishwanath (2014) further reiterates that not only are we checking our Facebook profiles regularly but also that we are creating multiple identities stating that "close to one in ten or approximately 100 million Facebook profile pages were duplicates or fake accounts" (p. 83), which is actually a practice forbidden by Facebook. Mentors and mentees are not excluded from this and what we can see in the Facebook sites is that there is potentiality for a conglomerate of regular Facebook posters posing both as mentees and mentors, depending upon which forum they are posting on or which identity they are using at the time. Vishwanath (2014) uses an example of a high school teacher posing as a student with the intention to retrieve sensitive information and details from the students. This therefore raises possibilities that beginning teachers could essentially be posing as experienced mentors whereas in reality their experience may be limited to a short professional life. In saying this, one then re-raises the question *what is a mentor and is this really a problem?* Despite already attempting to answer this in the introduction, we now stumble across a new phenomenon that challenges the traditional status and image of the mentor as the 'all-knowing' and 'wise one.' Instead, the mentor could either be posing as a mentor only in which the intentionality behind the image once again is seen as *I am a mentor because I am presenting myself as one*, or the mentor, whilst traditionally viewed 'mentee,' could genuinely be offering their experienced counterparts aspects of their acquired knowledge in contemporary early childhood theory, savvy ability in the use of social media and possible visionary status in embracing the pedagogical shift that has recently occurred in early childhood education. It could be argued then that the mentee is actually the mentor, however their wisdom has been compartmentalised to that which the traditional mentor may not have. On the other side of the coin we then see the mentors becoming the mentees, but what is interesting to note is their receptiveness to becoming seen as the mentee yet again after years of possibly being heralded as the mentor.

1.5 Social media and the early childhood teaching sector

In terms of this research, social media refers specifically to Social Networking Sites (SNS) that contain opportunities for teachers to share knowledge and views of early childhood education and care teaching pedagogy with a strong focus upon the opinions furnished to beginning teachers, with specific focus upon the use of Facebook. Whilst one could argue that networking through social media and the possible use of avatars challenges the notion of effective and authentic mentoring, social networking also provides the ability for educators to bond with their peers and develop knowledge of diversity, or reciprocate accepted norms of practice (Dennen & Myers, 2012).

Early childhood professional development organisations such as Early Childhood Australia, Gowrie Victoria and Community Child Care Victoria, make full usage of social media, specifically Facebook by providing access to services they offer, advertising and creating forums for discussions. The Commonwealth of Australia has also funded an online professional development program known as the *National Quality Standard Professional Learning Program* (NQS PLP) which has been developed and implemented by Early Childhood Australia (ECA). Whilst this program is considered a professional development program for all early childhood educators, new or experienced, it provides avenues for any member to comment or contribute to discussion. Another notable Australian online forum is the *Educators' Guide to Innovation Page* on Ning, which is a section of the *Innovate Here Online Community*, and hosted by the *Regional Services Group* of the Department of Education and Training, Victoria (formerly DEECD). For both of these online sites comments can be removed by moderators, although not before the potential damage may have been imposed.

In addition to sponsored online forums managed by professional agencies, early childhood educators alone can create forums or groups and add these to their Facebook page with the intention to demonstrate their work, seek guidance or offer their expertise and knowledge. On Facebook alone there is a significant number of early childhood closed group pages where Facebook members are invited, suggested or accepted on request by administrators who created the group. It is unknown as to whether these groups are mediated by professional academics or reputable early childhood leaders in the sector, yet there remains the potential to have a significant impact upon beginning teachers and the wider sector. Examples of early childhood Facebook groups include *ECA–NQS PLP Facebook Site* (now withdrawn from Facebook), *Beginning Early Childhood Teachers Victoria, Educational Leaders Unite, The Early Childhood Educators Place, Victorian Early Childhood Community, Educational Leaders Network and Support Group, Early Childhood Education, Educators that Care – a place for all early childhood professionals, Indigenous Perspectives in ECE – Wurundjeri Country, EYLF/NQF Ideas and Discussions* and *Early Childhood Teachers Victoria, Educators Engaging with Educators, Social Justice in Early Childhood* and the like. This is a small selection of what can be seen as a plethora of sites that have emerged seemingly with the intention to inspire and share knowledge and ideas with other early childhood educators.

Social media, in particular, Facebook provides a beginning teacher with instant mentoring which in turn has the potential to have a profound effect on the pedagogical practices and principles of educators in Australia. Whilst Smith Risser (2013) claims that seeking guidance through social media has existed for some time, previously in the form of online forums and community groups, social media sites such as Facebook and Twitter have taken over our nature of dialogue and forms of online connection that has diversified dialogue to include video, photographs and emojis or emoticons to implicate meaning or feelings. Emojis are a new pop culture phenomenon which are small icons representing an expression, action or feeling with emoticons mostly representing feelings. They can be used on SNS but also with various email platforms. Regardless of the platform, social media has provided a means of instant and available communication particularly with accessibility through smartphones. Despite the anticipation that advice might always be there, one might question the relevance and credibility of the advice given and from where it derives. It is therefore vital that beginning teachers develop skills in being able to make informed choices as to how they receive their mentoring and the validity of the mentoring given. To ensure quality mentoring through social media is consistently delivered, policy directives that incorporate strategic learning in pre-service training regimes may need to be considered.

Further literature associated specifically to mentoring through social media and the effects of this mentoring has become more prevalent of late, and is beginning to include how beginning teachers, in particular a younger generation of teachers, can connect with mentors through technology (Smith Risser, 2013). The benefits for using social media in mentoring include minimising costs and reaching mass numbers of mentees globally where knowledge can be shared and information gained (Colomo-Palacios et al., 2012). Further benefits include the ease of mentoring where communication is instant and not limited by geographic distances or the organisation of time to meet (Smith Risser, 2013). With the benefits, there also lies the risk of opening up unsolicited mentoring that has the potential to oppress pre-service teachers and/or beginning teachers as they grapple with their professional identity and efficacy (Galman, 2009; Hargreaves & Fullan, 2000; Macfarlane & Noble, 2005). In addition to this, there is also the danger of mentors becoming oppressed and challenged in their sense of efficacy both in teaching and mentoring through the publication of adverse responses to their initial suggestions and advice-giving. We also see the potential that posts and forums on Facebook may replace credible professional development (PD) as knowledge is gained, albeit superficially, instantly from consultants and professional development leaders online through their engagement with the Facebook forums. In saying this, accessing this type of PD through Facebook has its benefits if the knowledge and advice is from early childhood experts evidenced by rigorous research. Weigel, Weiser, Bales, and Moyses (2012), in their study of early childhood online users, suggest that internet usage was becoming favourable for educators to gain information and access professional development. Their study analysed the purpose of online professional development and how respondents preferred gaining instant access to information they could use immediately in their settings. Weigel et al. (2012) further concluded that the internet could very well be a positive tool for professional development for practitioners as it is instant and immediate. Use of social media or social networking at the time of their research however was not rated highly and most of the respondents found this to be too time-consuming. However, as time continues and various SNS platforms open up with further functionality, this pattern of behaviour may change.

Despite there being an increasing amount of literature regarding the use of social media in mentoring teachers, many of the articles relate to primary or secondary teaching as opposed to early childhood settings and not necessarily in an Australian context relating to recent early childhood legislative and pedagogical reforms. Furthermore, it is difficult to find specific Australian studies that directly involve mentoring or effects of *ad-hoc* mentoring through social media in relation to early childhood beginning teachers. This knowledge is particularly important as Australia currently suffers a shortage of early childhood teachers that is now required under new reforms and "more than a third of ECEC practitioners in Australia leave the field every year" (Fenech, 2013). In addition, one third of beginning teachers are likely to leave teaching for a variety of reasons (Tankersley, 2010) including burnout perhaps resulting from disillusionment of romanticised views of early childhood teaching (Macfarlane & Noble, 2005). This level of attrition creates even further dire circumstances for Australia's early childhood field and lack of teaching practitioners. Nolan and Rouse (2013) state that since the national early childhood reforms, early childhood teachers are in demand now more than ever before and therefore universities have been required to increase their places for students to cater for this need. They also state that despite the increase, university places have been marketed to appeal to potential students due to funding variations and as a result double degrees in both early childhood and primary teaching are now offered (Nolan & Rouse, 2013). Whilst this may benefit the increase in bachelor trained early childhood graduates available for education and care services, the harsh reality is that graduates are not necessary choosing early childhood as their career path. In their study which interviewed pre-service teachers from two universities, Nolan and Rouse (2013) found that double degree graduates are more likely to enter into the primary school profession rather than early childhood with reasons relating to pay, professional recognition and working conditions. Interestingly, their findings also indicated that professional placement held very strong motivators for their career preferences stating that participants "indicated that the placement and or the mentor teacher, in the placement setting, have the biggest influence on career aspirations" (p. 5). Once again this brings to the forefront the significance of mentoring in terms of both pre-service and graduate teacher attrition rates and likelihood to at least enter the early childhood field, let alone stay in it. Further questions emerge relating to the Facebook connections that pre-service teachers have with each other where they can share their placement experiences and discuss their motivation for merging into one sector or the other. Whilst it is a right for double degree pre-service teachers to choose their career path, could Facebook also be used to deter or attract pre-service teachers into the early childhood sector through pre-service and post-service mentoring by university trained experts? These questions are further explored in chapter five where further possibilities are suggested and discussed.

Aside from pre-service influences, the question still remains as to the motives or intentionality behind mentors using Facebook to mentor beginning teachers and how this impacts upon the mentees, now and in the future. Do they use Facebook purely to promote their ideas, thoughts and opinions and how does this actually influence the professional identify and efficacy of the graduate teacher? Does it really affect their career choice, progression or change as graduate teachers enter and/or move out of the field, or are they more resilient than given credit for and already know how to apply filters to their Facebook exploration? What we see also is a blurring of roles in terms of mentee and mentor and the possible altruistic identity that may lie beneath. Furthermore, what of the concept of gratification which is seen with the concept of 'instant advice' that is often readily available on Facebook early childhood forums? Returning to Vishwanath's (2014) discussion on motivations behind the obsessive nature of Facebook usage, this concept of gratification frequently emerges. The user's gratification heavily relies upon the nature in which the Facebook user utilises the platform, whether it is for social support, sharing of ideas or acknowledgement of skill and 'inspirations' from others. Therefore, in addition to the aforementioned arguments, mentorship can be seen as a *gratifying process*, both for the mentee and the mentor; however when it is instigated in an ad-hoc manner the gratification can be challenged and leave the mentee or mentor still yearning. In chapter four, I explore further the motivation behind the gratification to see if it appears to help others or help the 'self.' I question and explore the mentor's motivation behind their mentorship and if this is to receive gratification from public posts relating to the help they have given, or if they simply just want to help others. Once again, intentionality can be explored here as to the identity of the mentor and what makes them a mentor in terms of perception of self and perception from others. Before these discussions dig deeper into the online psyche of mentors and mentees, the methods in which these discussions were explored and analysed must be described, including how using a phenomenological approach opened lines of creativity in exploring data and depicting themes and where the initial collection of data has led to the larger study.

References

Aldwinckle, M. (2001). The DAP [Developmentally Appropriate Practice] debate: Are we throwing the baby out with the bath water? *Australian Journal of Early Childhood*, *26*(2), 36–39. Retrieved from http://search.informit.com.au.ezproxy.lib.monash.edu.au/documentSummary;dn=200112123;res=IELAPA

Allen, T. D., Shockley, K. M., & Poteat, L. (2010). Protégé anxiety attachment and feedback in mentoring relationships. *Journal of Vocational Behavior*, *77*(1), 73–80. doi:10.1016/j.jvb.2010.02.007

Anarchy and the EYLF Pirates. (2015). *Agency*. https://eylfpirates.wordpress.com/2015/01/20/agency/

Australian Children's Education and Care Quality Authority (ACECQA). (2013). *Guide to the National Quality Standard.* Retrieved 10 August, 2016, from http://files.acecqa.gov.au/files/ National-Quality-Framework-Resources-Kit/NQF03-Guide-toNQS-130902.pdf.

Baranik, L. E., Roling, E. A., & Eby, L. T. (2010). Why does mentoring work? The role of perceived organizational support. *Journal of Vocational Behavior*, *76*(3), 366–373. doi:10.1016/j.jvb.2009.07.004

Boyd, D. M., & Ellison, N. B. (2007). Social network sites: Definition, history, and scholarship. *Journal of Computer-Mediated Communication*, *13*(1), 210–230. doi:10.1111/j.1083-6101.2007.00393.x

Boyd, W. (2012). Maternal employment and childcare in Australia: Achievements and barriers to satisfying employment (Contributed Article). *Australian Bulletin of Labour*, *38*, 199+.

Campbell-Evans, G., Stamopoulos, E., & Maloney, C. (2014). Building leadership capacity in early childhood pre-service teachers. *Australian Journal of Teacher Education*, *39*(5), 41–49.

Cartmel, J., Macfarlane, K., & Noble, K. (2004). Pedagogy in the nursery: Establishing practitioner partnerships in high-quality long day care programs. *Australian Journal of Early Childhood, 29*, 38+.

Cheeseman, S., Sumsion, J., & Press, F. (2014). Infants of the knowledge economy: The ambition of the Australian government's early years learning framework. *Pedagogy, Culture & Society, 22*(3), 405–424. doi:10.1080/14681366.2014.914967

Chryssochoou, X. (2003). Studying identity in social psychology. *Journal of Language & Politics, 2*(2), 225–241.

Colomo-Palacios, R., Casado-Lumbreras, C., Soto-Acosta, P., & Misra, S. (2012). Providing knowledge recommendations: An approach for informal electronic mentoring. *Interactive Learning Environments, 22*(2), 221–240. doi:10.1080/10494820.2012.745430

Coombe, K. (2011). *Early Childhood Education Workforce Capacity Project: Mentoring for the Reflective Early Childhood Practitioner.* NSW: CSU Print.

Copple, C., & Bredekamp, S. (2008). Getting clear about developmentally appropriate practice. *YC Young Children, 63*(1), 54–55. doi:10.2307/42730228

Crowell, S. (2013). *Normativity and phenomenology in Husserl and Heidegger*. New York: Cambridge University Press.

Cummins, L. (2004). The pot of gold at the end of the rainbow: Mentoring in early childhood education. *Childhood Education, 80*, 254+.

Dennen, V. P., & Myers, J. B. (2012). *Virtual professional development and informal learning via social networks*. Hershey, PA: IGI Global.

Department of Education & Training (DET). (2017). *Mentor training for experienced early childhood teachers.* http://www.education.vic.gov.au/Documents/childhood/professionals/profdev/EMPFactSheetandFAQ.pdf

Desimone, L. M., Hochberg, E. D., Porter, A. C., Polikoff, M. S., Schwartz, R., & Johnson, L. J. (2014). Formal and informal mentoring: Complementary, compensatory, or consistent? *Journal of Teacher Education, 65*(2), 88–110. doi:10.1177/0022487113511643

Dunham-Taylor, J., Lynn, C. W., Moore, P., McDaniel, S., & Walker, J. K. (2008). What goes around comes around: Improving faculty retention through more effective mentoring. *Journal of Professional Nursing, 24*(6), 337–346. doi:10.1016/j.profnurs.2007.10.013

Dunn, M., Harrison, L. J., & Coombe, K. (2008). In good hands: Preparing research-skilled graduates for the early childhood profession. *Teaching and Teacher Education, 24*(3), 703–714. doi:10.1016/j.tate.2007.09.002

Eller, L. S., Lev, E. L., & Feurer, A. (2014). Key components of an effective mentoring relationship: A qualitative study. *Nurse Education Today, 34*(5), 815–820. doi:10.1016/j.nedt.2013.07.020

Fajet, W., Bello, M., Leftwich, S. A., Mesler, J. L., & Shaver, A. N. (2005). Pre-service teachers' perceptions in beginning education classes. *Teaching and Teacher Education, 21*(6), 717–727. doi:10.1016/j.tate.2005.05.002

Fenech, S. (2013). Leadership development during times of reform. *Australasian Journal of Early Childhood, 38*, 89+.

Ferris, S. P., & Wilder, H. A. (2013). *The plugged-in professor: Tips and techniques for teaching with social media.* Oxford, UK: Chandos Publishing.

Fleer, M. (2005). Developmental fossils – Unearthing the artefacts of early childhood education: The reification of 'Child Development'. *Australian Journal of Early Childhood, 30*, 2+.

Galman, S. (2009). Doth the lady protest too much? Pre-service teachers and the experience of dissonance as a catalyst for development. *Teaching and Teacher Education, 25*(3), 468–481. doi:10.1016/j.tate.2008.08.002

Garvis, S. (2011). An exploratory investigation on the influence of practical experience towards shaping future early childhood teachers' practice in the arts. *Australasian Journal of Early Childhood, 36*(3), 117–121.

Giovacco-Johnson, T. (2011). Applied ethics as a foundation in early childhood teacher education: Exploring the connections and possibilities. *Early Childhood Education Journal, 38*(6), 449–456.

Good, K. D. (2012). From scrapbook to Facebook: A history of personal media assemblage and archives. *New Media & Society, 15*(4), 557–573. doi:10.1177/1461444812458432

Grondin, J. (2005). Why reawaken the question of being? In R. Polt (Ed.), *Heidegger's being and time: Critical essays*. Maryland: Rowman and Littlefield Publishers, Inc.

Hall, J. A., Pennington, N., & Lueders, A. (2014). Impression management and formation on Facebook: A lens model approach. *New Media & Society, 16*(6), 958–982. doi:10.1177/1461444813495166

Hallam, P. R., Chou, P. N., Hite, J. M., & Hite, S. J. (2012). Two contrasting models for mentoring as they affect retention of beginning teachers. *National Association of Secondary School Principals. NASSP Bulletin, 96*(3), 243–278.

Hargreaves, A., & Fullan, M. (2000). Mentoring in the new millennium. *Theory Into Practice, 39*(1), 50.

Hurd, N., & Zimmerman, M. (2014). An analysis of natural mentoring relationship profiles and associations with mentees' mental health: Considering links via support from important others. *American Journal of Community Psychology, 53*(1–2), 25–36. doi:10.1007/s10464-013-9598-y

Inspired EC. (2014). '*Tis the Season... to Abandon our Philosophy?*' https://inspiredec.com.au/tis-the-season-to-abandon-our-philosophy/

Jordan, T. (2013). *Internet, society and culture: Communicative practices before and after the Internet*. Edited by K. D. Good. New York: Bloomsbury Academic.

Kaun, A., & Stiernstedt, F. (2014). Facebook time: Technological and institutional affordances for media memories. *New Media & Society, 16*(7), 14. doi:10.1177/1461444814544001

Kietzmann, J. H., Hermkens, K., McCarthy, I. P., & Silvestre, B. S. (2011). Social media? Get serious! Understanding the functional building blocks of social media. *Business Horizons, 54*(3), 241–251. doi:10.1016/j.bushor.2011.01.005

Koç, E. M. (2012). Idiographic roles of cooperating teachers as mentors in pre-service distance teacher education. *Teaching and Teacher Education, 28*(6), 818–826. doi:10.1016/j.tate.2012.03.007

Loizou, E. (2011). The diverse facets of power in early childhood mentor – Student teacher relationships. *European Journal of Teacher Education, 34*(4), 373–386. doi:10.1080/02619768.2011.587112

Macfarlane, K., & Noble, K. (2005). Romance or reality? Examining burnout in early childhood teachers. *Australian Journal of Early Childhood, 30*, 53+.

McCartin, J., Nolan, A. & Beahan, J. (2014). Professional mentoring program for Early Childhood Teachers: Final Report Cohort 3 December 2013 Project Report. Melbourne, Victoria: Department of Education & Early Childhood Development.

Nailon, D. (2013). Researching ECEC professional development: Using Kelly's repertory grid to examine changes in educators' constructs about curriculum design in early childhood settings. *Australasian Journal of Early Childhood, 38*, 81+.

Nolan, A., & Rouse, E. (2013). Where to from here? Career choices of pre-service teachers undertaking a dual early childhood/primary qualification [online]. *Australian Journal of Teacher Education (Online), 38*(1), 1–10.

Nolan, A., & Sim, J. (2011). Exploring and evaluating levels of reflection in pre-service early childhood teachers. *Australasian Journal of Early Childhood, 36*(3), 122–130.

Nosheen Rachel, N. (2013). Peer mentoring: Enhancing social cohesion in Pakistani universities. *Higher Education, Skills and Work – Based Learning, 3*(2), 130–140. doi:10.1108/20423891311313162

Ockenden, W. (2015, 16 August). How your phone tracks your every move. *ABC News*. Retrieved from www.abc.net.au/news/2015-08-16/metadata-retention-privacy-phone-will-ockenden/6694152

O'Neill, S., & Stephenson, J. (2012). Exploring Australian pre-service teachers sense of efficacy, its sources, and some possible influences. *Teaching and Teacher Education, 28*(4), 535–545. doi:10.1016/j.tate.2012.01.008

Ortlipp, M., Arthur, L., & Woodrow, C. (2011). Discourses of the early years learning framework: Constructing the early childhood professional. *Contemporary Issues in Early Childhood, 12*(1), 56–70. doi:10.2304/ciec.2011.12.1.56

Ortlipp, M., & Nuttall, J. (2011). Supervision and assessment of the early childhood practicum: Experiences of pre-service teachers who speak English as a second language and their supervising teachers. *Australasian Journal of Early Childhood, 36*(2), 87–94.

Poldre, P. (1994). Mentoring programs: A question of design. *Interchange, 25*(2), 183–193. doi:10.1007/BF01534544

Polt, R. (2005). *Heidegger's Being and Time: Critical Essays*. Maryland, USA: MD: Rowman and Littlefield Publishers, INC.

Ross, C., Orr, E. S., Sisic, M., Arseneault, J. M., Simmering, M. G., & Orr, R. R. (2009). Personality and motivations associated with Facebook use. *Computers in Human Behavior, 25*(2), 578–586. doi:10.1016/j.chb.2008.12.024

Rothwell, W. J., & Chee, P. (2013). *Becoming an Effective Mentoring Leader.* New York City, USA: McGraw-Hill.

Sanfey, H., Hollands, C., & Gantt, N. L. (2013). Strategies for building an effective mentoring relationship. *The American Journal of Surgery, 206*(5), 714–718. doi:10.1016/j.amjsurg.2013.08.001

Semann, A. (2015). *Lets talk about etiquette: Facebook and beyond.* http://semannslattery.com/lets-talk-about-etiquette-facebook-and-beyond/

Smith Risser, H. (2013). Virtual induction: A novice teacher's use of Twitter to form an informal mentoring network. *Teaching and Teacher Education, 35*, 25–33. doi:10.1016/j.tate.2013.05.001

Stamopou[illegible] (2012). Reframing early childhood leadership. *Australasian Journal of Early Childhood, 37*, 42+.

Tankersley, A. A. (2010). Discovering curriculum concerns of beginning early childhood teachers. *Childhood Education, 86*, 293+.

Telecommunications (Interception and Access) Amendment (Data Retention) Act 2015, Commonwealth of Australia, 39 Stat. (ComLaw 2015 13 April 2015).

Tucker, H. (2015, 13 October). New data retention laws begin today, this is what you need to know. *News.com.au*. Retrieved from www.news.com.au/technology/online/new-data-retention-laws-begin-today-this-is-what-you-need-to-know/news-story/28ea2dc1b01d15e53f474e21b6d68501

van Dijck, J. (2013). *The culture of connectivity: A critical history of social media*. New York: Oxford University Press.

Vanwynsberghe, H., & Verdegem, P. (2013). Integrating social media in education. *Comparative Literature and Culture, 15*(3). Retrieved from http://docs.lib.purdue.edu/clcweb/vol15/iss3/10. doi:10.7771/1481-4374.2247

Vishwanath, A. (2014, August 3). Habitual Facebook use and its impact on getting deceived on social media. *Journal of Computer-Mediated Communication, 20*, 83–98. doi:10.1111/jcc4.12100

Walkington, J. (2005). Mentoring preservice teachers in the preschool setting: Perceptions of the role. *Australian Journal of Early Childhood, 30*, 28+.

Weigel, D. J., Weiser, D. A., Bales, D. W., & Moyses, K. J. (2012). Identifying online preferences and needs of early childhood professionals. *Early Childhood Research & Practice, 14*.

Whitehead, K., & Krieg, S. (2013). 'Herstories': Using an historical lens to examine continuities and changes in early childhood teacher education. *Australasian Journal of Early Childhood, 38*(4), 8.

Wisnewski, J. J. (2013). *Heidegger: An introduction*. Maryland, USA: Rowman and Littlefield Publishers, Inc.

2 Exploring the problem

2.1 The exploration

The larger research study explored the perceptions Australian early childhood beginning teachers have concerning the informal mentoring they have received from peers and colleagues through social media and if this has affected them in their teaching practices and workforce retention. More specifically, this particular aspect of the study investigated the online perceptions of early childhood beginning teachers regarding what they believe to be best practice in early childhood education settings and how this might have changed, both positively and negatively in response to the challenges or support from informal mentoring through online social networking. This exploration further considered possible consequences to the way mentoring through Facebook was delivered, including conduct of both mentors and mentees and how this may impact upon the daily discussions and rhetoric between the two. The purpose of exploring these online interactions was to discover the level of impact they may have had upon the beginning teacher's sense of efficacy particularly in their transition from student to teacher which was observed through their response or lack of response. The research also explored and discussed the particular topics that attracted debate and whether or not the manner in which the topic was debated appeared to be professional or unprofessional. These findings are analysed to determine the possible impact they might be having upon the beginning teacher and possibly even mentor teachers.

2.2 Phenomenology

In gaining depth and specific detail relating to the effects of social media on beginning teachers, a phenomenological approach has been used, stemming from an epistemology of constructionism, whereby the researcher and participants construct meaning and thematic concepts through their interaction with the world (Gray, 2014). Phenomenology enabled the data to be analysed in terms of studying a phenomenon, which in this case was mentoring through social media, specifically Facebook. Researcher immersion gave meaning and depth to understanding this phenomenon and its prevalence and impact on the beginning teacher's professional life. Whilst the researcher could not be there in the room with the beginning teacher experiencing or observing the effects of the impact, she could however observe the written reaction through recording and analysing social media threads and posts. Zingale (2013), in his article on phenomenological studies, questions whether one has the ability to share perspectives without actually being in the same situation or location at the time. He also illuminates that whilst we are able to sift through the reels of advice, he questions "how the networker is able to tell what to disregard and what appears meaningful?" (p. 291). Applied to this study, one could question how beginning teachers were able to sift through bad advice from self-promoted mentors from the solid and authentic advice from professional mentors? Which advice was meaningful and which advice has an element of self-promotion for the mentor? Furthermore, which type of mentoring approach embedded an element of condescending tones to deter the beginning teacher from continuing to participate or post comments themselves?

Zingale (2013) brings us back to the work of Martin Heidegger with a powerful notion of *de-situation*. This concept arises strongly in the use of social media as it asserts that communication through this means is not whole and is based upon the speakers' perception or concept of truth that they want to be shared. "The assertion can be something that is retold but, because the retold assertion has been decontextualized, it can only carry a partial meaning of what is relevant to the practical activity" (p. 291). In the context of this study, social media provides a platform of being physically absent from the conceptual understanding of the notion, or question from experience. They are therefore unable to truly share in the experience, but may be able to relate the phenomenon through their own experiences they may have had. In terms of the beginning teachers and their receipt of mentoring through social media, one may assume that the beginning teacher may not have had the experience as guided by the mentor, and therefore is not only de-situated from the advice, but is unable to directly relate in a whole form. Whilst the use of imagination and assumption may be prevalent with the retelling of the story as it passes on to other beginning teachers, there is still the potential to lose its authenticity and relevance.

Zingale (2013) also refers to the concept of *telling*. How is it that a person can tell what is and what is not through a description of another's perception of an incident or advice? Unless the person has direct involvement with the incident or advice described, one cannot assume that they can judge accurately. This is also applicable to the mentor as they take from the beginning teacher a version of the situation from the beginning teacher's perspective and understanding, and base their advice on written posts without context of others, physical surroundings and absolute sequence of events.

It was therefore beneficial to use phenomenological methodology to be able to closely study each situation as it presented itself including potential displacement or de-situation. It was also important to ascertain the potential to lose context in the mentoring and possible prevalence of self-promotion of the mentor at the expense of the beginning teacher. This was used to then explore if this conduct contributed to the possible reasons as to why beginning teachers may have lost confidence in their ability within the first year of teaching, and even perhaps why they may have considered leaving the profession altogether.

Researcher as participant

According to Gray (2014), phenomenology is particularly useful in exploring constructs and perspectives arising from groups who engage in common experiences, such as teaching in early childhood. As the researcher, the methods of immersing myself in the dialogue between beginning teachers and mentors has allowed me to consider and understand their particular paradigm and use this to explore what constitutes both helpful mentoring and that which one may consider a hindrance. Furthermore, I have a strong interest both in the pursuit of maintaining quality teachers in the profession and the fascination of Facebook as it incessantly enters the daily lives of teachers. I have been working in the early years' sector for over two decades and during this time have seen a shift in pedagogy and practice in early childhood settings, accompanied by what seems to be a rising level of anxiety and apprehension in teachers. Recently, this has been particularly noticeable in beginning teachers who are looking for guidance from experienced teachers, yet to find their mentors also experiencing confusion. During the change in legislation and the introduction of the National Quality Framework, I worked as Assistant Manager at DET (formerly DEECD) and spent a good deal of time listening to teachers in the sector express their concerns and confusion at network meetings and presentations. This also raised arguments amongst colleagues. Furthermore, I am a regular user of social media, especially Facebook, both now in my role as an early childhood consultant and for personal uses.

Over the last year or so, I have noticed a rise in personal attacks between colleagues when discussing philosophical and pedagogical beliefs on social media sites. In parallel to this, there have also been many comments or requests for mercy and consideration in posts, asking responders not to attack or engage in abusive conduct. At times, I have seen that abusive conduct has resulted in members leaving the forums and therefore become limited in their ability to seek guidance and mentorship through these easily accessible sites. As a result, my curiosity and concern for the sector in their professional identity and efficacy has been significantly raised. This experience has motivated my passion towards researching current mentoring practices and exploring possibilities of more structured and systematic mentoring for beginning teachers. Immersing myself fully within the research method provided an avenue to experience first-hand the receipt of mentoring, including at times verbal abuse and insult, hence becoming the researcher participant in this phenomenological study of mentoring in social media.

Research design using phenomenological methods

To begin to understand and discover why it was necessary to fully immerse myself into the informal mentoring world that beginning teachers were experiencing, I refer more specifically to the methods of phenomenology and how the constructs evolve within this process. Smith, Flowers, and Larkin (2009) refer to the works of Husserl, a founding philosopher in phenomenological studies who believed that experiencing the phenomenon by one's self would give the researcher fundamental insight into the elements of the experience. If I wanted to discover the current topics of contention and debate, and the very nature of mentoring as it occurred on Facebook, I needed to enter the discussion in an authentic manner, both as an observer and a contributor, mindfully ensuring that my contributions did not influence conduct of the process of discussion. By taking this approach, I was able to give possibility to the discovery of current topics that produced ongoing debate or controversy, investigate how brazen or sensitive mentors and mentees were as they engaged in this style of mentoring and how the discussions could potentially make the mentee feel about their professional identity and practice as a teacher. Specifically, I observed and recorded comments and responses posted on a Facebook pages that had limited moderation and heightened freedom of speech. At times, I would also comment, albeit in moderation so as not to strongly influence many discussions or pages in heated dialogue. This gave me the first-hand experience of both supportive mentoring, but also condescending comments, with some particularly targeted to my posts, rather than the discussion itself.

The main pages used were Facebook forum group sites, whereby members were either invited to join or asked to join with administrators of the particular group making decisions about user permissions. These Facebook forum group sites were selected according to the purpose of discussion of the group and were specifically related to early childhood education in

Australia with a focus and attraction to first year beginning (graduate) early childhood teachers. Whilst this was the intention, it was at times difficult to ascertain who was the mentor and who was the beginning teacher. This meant that I had to delve further into the contributors' public profiles with most successfully determined; yet others remained uncertain. The analysis included observing patterns of posts and establishing issues of contention that had the potential to negatively and positively impact upon the beginning teacher. With this, I looked for responses that could either indicate submission to the mentor's viewpoint, responses defending the mentee's viewpoint or withdrawal from the dialogue altogether. Detailed field notes of observation in this research provided a method for greater understanding of the techniques, styles of conversation and nature of uses of these particular sites. This information was used to inform the nature of discussion and questions conducted in the semi-structured forums.

Methods

In the overall research, I have used a mixed-methods approach, focussing upon qualitative data and utilising quantitative data to validate findings and extend knowledge. Historically, social science academics have borrowed and used research methods from the scientific community, however there is now question as to what is considered to be *clean data* (Manjikian, 2013). Whilst qualitative methods alone may not have received absolute credibility, using only quantitative methods may have also imposed restrictions regarding the gathering and analysing of contextual data and depth of meaning behind the findings. Flick, Garms-Homolová, Herrmann, Kuck, and Röhnsch (2012) argue that mixed-methods are not used for validity alone, but also to extend and deepen knowledge gained from the research. Gray (2014) further explains that mixed-methods enable "researchers to generalize from a sample to a population and to gain a richer, contextual understanding of the phenomenon being researched" (Gray, 2014, p. 194). My intent in the overall research was to use qualitative methods under a phenomenological approach to establish and develop constructs that were then used to apply to a wider selection of participants through statistical data collection. The constructs were therefore not known until the first two phases of data collection had been completed and the themes emerging from these phases had been developed. Gray (2014) also implies that using qualitative methods first followed by quantitative methods is particularly relevant for studies where little is known about the setting or problems to be researched. It was therefore applicable for the overall investigation to sequentially evolve as whilst there is research in mentoring early childhood teachers, and also studies completed relating to mentoring through social media, there is little known about how informal mentoring impacts upon beginning early childhood teachers through informal mentoring. Constructs are discovered throughout all of the phases with common themes and new themes emerging in each phase. The flexibility of the study also included immersing myself as the researcher into the field with the intention to understand the uses of social media by early childhood beginning teachers and informal mentors within a phenomenological methodology.

The methods that took the form of a phenomenological approach included the following two groups of data sets: (1) a Facebook page analysis and (2) semi-structured interviews with beginning teachers and teaching mentors, whilst the third data set was purely qualitative being a national online survey. In this initial phase, inductive reasoning was used to code and to eventually build more effectively across the three qualitative data sets a theoretical case of early childhood mentoring practices, as they currently exist through social media. Gray (2014) suggests that whilst quantitative data collection methods aim to validate an hypothetical theory, inductive reasoning within qualitative research methods focusses upon establishing the theory in the first place, based upon an unknown. Thematic analysis then explored concepts of both latent and manifest data as well as some statistical data relating to frequency of requests for legislative knowledge and advice on professional practice.

Links to the rest of the research

In terms of linking this initial phase to the remainder of the larger research study, deductive measures were used through quantitative data collection to confirm or deny the prevalence of theory as evolved in the qualitative processes and determine variables whilst inductive reasoning has been used here to ascertain interpretation of the early childhood Facebook forum conversations. Using mixed-methods has therefore allowed for two processes; firstly, to establish the theory through the analysis of qualitative data and secondly to verify it through statistical data collection methods. In addition to this verification, the statistical data aimed to provide further insight into the current status of early childhood teachers, both beginning and mentors and their sense of efficacy in the current climate of legislative and pedagogical change in Australia. It is this analysis that gives depth and rationale behind action to support beginning teachers more effectively and meaningfully in their career advancement. The findings and analysis of the findings of the initial phase for this book relate only to data set one being the Facebook page analysis as previously described, however further significant links are made with the second set of data collected, being the semi-structured interviews.

Justification of using phenomenology in mixed-methods

Whilst the use of phenomenology is not normally used in mixed-methods approaches, there have been instances where this method has been successfully applied and seen as an innovative way to expand the designs of research that are usually founded in one approach. Mayoh and Onwuegbuzie (2015) consider that phenomenological research methods can be applied well due to its flexible and adaptable nature and expands research methodology in a way that is enriching and incorporative of philosophical aspects. This means that certain components of the research study apply phenomenological methods alone to allow for unstructured collection of data and analysis forming future directions of questioning that then can be explored through more structured quantitative methods. In terms of this research, phenomenology allowed the researcher to engage in the lived experience of the evidence, being a participator in Facebook, posting, responding and watching and could therefore use this evidence to form further questions that could be explored through a wider audience such as the national survey. More specifically, interpretive phenomenology is applicable in the qualitative method of this research which is why the works of Heidegger were drawn upon. In terms of process, Mayoh and Onwuegbuzie (2015) suggest that moving "sequentially between qualitative and quantitative methods carries great potential as qualitative methods naturally set the stage for quantitative research used in an explanatory manner to test theories developed through phenomenological inquiry" (p. 100). In this case, the discovery of conceptual ideas arising from the online analysis of Facebook engagement provides a foundation of inquiry for the interviews and finally the online survey.

Participants

Posts from approximately 36 Facebook members across various sites were selected to use as an initial foundation for gathering data. This data was specifically aimed at discovering the nature of usage, demographic of participants and typical posts and threads published on Facebook. The selection of participants was not limited to community-based or privately owned organisations, but was inclusive of both as well as independent schools and in fact at times was difficult to ascertain exactly the type of workplace setting the member was employed in, which may have extended to members working in local or state governments, universities, consultancy firms and non-government organisations (NGO) such as not-for-profit kindergarten cluster management organisations. Participants were located from all areas of Australia and were not limited to any particular state or territory; however it became evident through introductory posts from participants that many were from Victoria in some groups, particularly those aimed at Victorian members such as the Early Childhood Teachers Victoria forum. Forum groups or sites were not purposely selected, but were randomised; however member participants from each group fulfilled the criteria of having some sort of early childhood qualifications at a tertiary level. This ranged from certificate 3 in children's services through to those with a doctorate. All participants were active users of social media and regularly applied their mentoring skills or were observed to be in receipt of mentoring through this medium. In the remainder of the larger investigation 6 individual participants qualified with a bachelor degree or above were recruited for semi-structured interviews, which was followed by a nationwide survey attracting 102 participants. The participants at each level included qualified teachers who are currently working in the sector in some way, either in long day care settings, early learning centres as part of a larger independent or government school or community-based sessional preschools.

It is important at this stage to acknowledge that the Facebook pages chosen included both public and closed groups and therefore careful, ethical procedures were developed and maintained to protect the identity of those who were participating in the discussions on the Facebook threads. Comments used for analysis were therefore removed from any form of publishing in this monograph and all participants were de-identified during the coding process and given a number so that their posts across several sites could be analysed without revealing who they were or whether they were an administrator (admin) of the group or how long they had worked in the field. The only particular information utilised in this research was the evidence of usage across sites as well as whether they acted on that site as a mentee or a mentor or possibly both; however this was for the purpose of analysis only and not to provide detail of the member's comments. Facebook requires consent to reproduce comments from specific users; however for the protection of Facebook users, I decided not to include them, but rather describe the discussions, nature of engagement and emotionality of the discussion. Copyright explanations given on behalf of Facebook often referred to works of art, photographs and music; however to protect the intellectual property (in addition to their identity) of the networkers/ members I have not reproduced any such statement, photo or quote for this publication. Human ethics approval was granted to conduct the research for the overall study which included exploring posts made on Facebook forums that are discussed here, data collected through interviews and findings of the nationwide survey that are explored in additional publications.

Thematic analysis

In determining the key ideas that emerged from this initial phase of the study, thematic analysis was used. Given that this investigation is a phenomenology, thematic analysis was most appropriate in deciphering through the latent and manifest meaning behind the data as well as the naturally occurring themes in threads and across pages. Using a thematic approach allowed me to engage solidarity into the theme, concluding that it was something that was co-ordinating itself into a pattern of validity. According to Gray (2014) thematic analysis enables patterns and themes to be identified and analysed within the qualitative data of the investigation. Themes utilised are those that emerge and specifically hold significant meaning to the findings where inferences and conclusions could be made that directly relate to the overarching research questions and pathways of investigation (Gray, 2014). Themes also can vary in their frequency and intensity and therefore the analysis and dissection of these themes strengthen their importance and significance in the research. It was therefore applicable for this particular study to uncover the underlying themes and trends of Facebook usage, discussions and influences for two reasons:

1. To establish a sound knowledge base in what is actually going on with regards to mentoring through Facebook and the key nature of engagement as well as significant topics of discussions that created interest or debate; and secondly in relation to the larger research project,
2. To discover if these were making an impact upon the professional self-efficacy of beginning teachers and their daily practice and whether or not this encouraged or discouraged them to remain in the field.

In terms of this particular section of the research, it is the first reason that remains as the key purpose for using thematic analysis both in discovering themes and in discussing findings from the Facebook page examination. This also provides strength and stability as the emergence of themes is linked to a central concept of professional efficacy and mentorship relationships and interactions. Nvivo was used as a coding software program to sort the data into themes that could be further analysed both within this data set and through triangulation with the data sets to come in the larger research project. I searched for patterns that were significant in terms of the impact they might have had on the participant also recalling how some comments previously had impacted upon me when I was engaging with others on Facebook. The coding process used inductive reasoning, with an expectation that recurrent themes and patterns may emerge from the data at this stage and evolve and change as the study developed. Inductive reasoning allowed for the concepts of 'likeliness' to occur rather than 'factually' occurring, as Facebook is only one portion of a person's life and also it is not certain that the profile presented on Facebook is truly that of the participant in reality. It is through this approach that the findings began to provide clues in forming answers to the overall research question, which will now be described in chapter three.

References

Flick, U., Garms-Homolová, V., Herrmann, W. J., Kuck, J., & Röhnsch, G. (2012). 'I can't prescribe something just because someone asks for it . . .': Using mixed methods in the framework of triangulation. *Journal of Mixed Methods Research, 6*(2), 97–110. doi:10.1177/1558689812437183

Gray, D. E. (2014). *Doing research in the real world.* 3rd ed. Los Angeles, CA: SAGE.

Manjikian, M. (2013). Positivism, post-positivism, and intelligence analysis. *International Journal of Intelligence and CounterIntelligence*, *26*(3), 563–582. doi:10.1080/08850607.2013.758002

Mayoh, J., & Onwuegbuzie, A. J. (2015). Toward a conceptualization of mixed methods phenomenological research. *Journal of Mixed Methods Research*, *9*(1), 91–107. doi:10.1177/1558689813505358

Smith, J. A., Flowers, P., & Larkin, M. (2009). *Interpretive phenomenological analysis: Theory, method and research.* London: SAGE Publications Ltd.

Zingale, N. C. (2013). The phenomenology of sharing: Social media networking, asserting, and telling. *Journal of Public Affairs*, *13*(3), 288–297. doi:10.1002/pa.1468

3 What is actually happening on Facebook?

In this chapter, I focus upon the analysis of the initial data set, its influence upon the sequence of the collection of the remaining data sets and the implications of the findings so far in terms of what is actually happening of Facebook. Using a phenomenological approach to the collection of this data, I explain the emerging themes that have arisen at this initial stage and how this appears to be impacting upon beginning teachers in their practices.

Revealing the phenomenon

Using this approach has allowed me to collect the data in an unstructured manner and record subjective perspectives from participants, despite the sequencing of data sets. The freedom of phenomenology also allowed me to explore and discover findings that were outside the research question, giving depth to the current positioning of early childhood teachers' current sense of efficacy and manner of interactions with each other (Gray, 2014). Gray argues that whilst the phenomenological approach can produce 'thick descriptions' giving richness to the data, this can sometimes be seen as minimising impartiality of the study, which is why other forms of analysis, including triangulation have been used in the overall study. Furthermore, I was able to use phenomenology in light of philosopher Husserl's construct of "experiential content of consciousness . . . (focussing) on each and every particular thing in its own right" (Smith, Flowers & Larkin, 2009, loc. 209). As an immersed researcher, and a member of the forum groups, I was able to see and experience each aspect of the dialogue unfolding which along with it came underlying possibilities of emotion that needed further analysis to decipher.

In the overall research, inductive reasoning is used to code and to eventually build more effectively across the three qualitative data sets, a theoretical case of early childhood mentoring practices, as they currently exist through social media. Gray (2014) suggests that whilst quantitative data collection methods aim to validate an hypothetical theory, inductive reasoning within qualitative research methods focus upon establishing the theory in the first place, based upon an unknown. Thematic analysis in this phase has explored concepts of both latent and manifest data as well as some thematic data relating to the types of requests for information and advice on legislation and professional practice. What was surprising was the variance of posts that were made across a series of pages by the same members regardless of whether they considered themselves a mentor or a mentee.

3.1 Analysis of Facebook pages

The analyses of the Facebook pages were conducted over a series of months dating from June 2014 to January 2015 and revisited in March 2016. This provided for opportunities to capture key discussions over time and threads of dialogue that members contributed to, debated against and offered advice both in written text and through visual photographs and videos. Revisiting this a year later also strengthened the continued existence of these discussions and revealed both the lack of or possible increased need for gratification from mentors and mentees and the frustrations they continued to experience in the sector through this medium. The purpose of the analysis was to gather how frequently beginning teachers contributed or responded to discussions and the manner in which they responded. Furthermore, it was to explore the topics of discussion that seemed to cause deeper reflection of the teachers as well as any emerging themes and responses both negative and positive. Whilst initially the plan was to capture a small time frame of online posts I quickly realised that certain topics had historical value and therefore prompted me to go back further to explore the discussions and dialogue that has taken place over an extended period of time and to explore additional dialogue expressing knowledge and opinion of these topics. It was also important to revisit the topics over 12 months later to see if they were still bouncing around as an issue or if there had been some sector resolve and effectual ease of the issues. Therefore, whilst the main threads were captured within specific time frames, some samples of dialogue have also been taken throughout 2014, 2015 and 2016. Establishing the nature of discussions upon these sites aimed to assist with the variables between helpful mentoring and condescending mentoring. This was usually established in the manner of responses, considering that direct responses and the actual meaning behind the response may service two varying possibilities.

The pages selected for analysis included both closed and public forums to which any identifying material was discarded to protect the identity of the members, particularly for the closed forum groups in which I had been granted permission to be a member of. Closed group forums are designed to minimise public viewing and therefore have certain procedures in joining the group. Most closed groups require an element of 'permission' whereby members can either request to join or be invited to join by the forum administrator/s. The forum administrator/s are usually those who have established the group or perhaps one member has developed the group and invited others to assist with administration. Many of the pages began with a pinned post that described the rules of the posting and the purpose of the group. Rules generally include determining the code of conduct and ethical behaviour that should be observed when posting; however at times these elements were not included. Often a second pinned post would include members introducing themselves, their roles, qualifications and sometimes which suburb or township they lived and/or taught in. Administrator behaviour varied across the group pages with some imposing strict rules and observances of courteous speech, whilst others declared that they would not remove threads or conversations as a courtesy to the ubiquitous concept of 'freedom of speech.' In the pages chosen for this research administrators appeared to be mostly qualified in some way in early childhood education; however it could not be determined that all had trained to the level of a bachelor degree.

Other patterns of behaviour I observed were the frequency of posts by specific members and the nature of their post. At times, members called out for advice, whilst other times they would like to challenge a philosophical construct, and again at other times they generally requested to just 'have a rant.' In determining who the frequent members were, I utilised the pinned post where members could introduce themselves, their qualifications and/or experience, as well as where they were from. Patterns of behaviour also included the types of language used and ethical practices that were or were not adhered to, implicating a lack or prevalence of professional decorum on the sites. This is discussed in more detail further within the analysis.

The concept of latent versus manifest meaning can also be applied to whether mentoring is helpful or condescending, depending upon the nature of the post and response, and from whom the response comes. The concept of de-situation appears strongly apparent here, where members enjoy the freedom of posting at their convenience or 'moment in time.' Therefore, the member in whom the response may or may not refer to at times appears confused at the underlying tone and inference of the post. This has led to debates, arguments and at times members leaving the group.

3.2 Latent versus manifest data from dialogue-in-text

Barbour and Schostak (2011) discuss the interpretation of dialogue when interviewing and conducting forums with participants which can be applied here in the case of analysing Facebook dialogue. They discuss the hidden issues that can be associated with these forms of methods, including acknowledgement of latent meaning behind statements or underlying truths that provide an alternative perspective or message in addition to the literal words posted (Barbour & Schostak, 2011). Gray (2014) stipulates that analysing meaning from dialogue requires the researcher to go deeper than interpreting literal contexts in order to make connections between dialogue that has been broken down into smaller components. By using this approach, it became further possible to see underlying connections of meaning across themes discussed as well as the manner in which it was discussed. For example, members who discussed their pedagogical approaches in teaching also described this approach through the manner in which they documented their planning. One particular thread argued about the lack of thought put into the learning that occurred in experiences and a particular member was frustrated at the focus upon the successfulness of the activities, rather than the learning that occurred in them. They were particularly annoyed at the focus of documentation in relation to following up where the focus had been more on the way the educator had interacted, rather than on how the child learnt. They further argued that teaching should be about being *in the moment* rather than always thinking about what to do next. They also included provocative statements relating to the assessment and rating process, hinting that they would ask authorised officers (who were assessing their practice in relation to quality), to leave if they challenged their version of quality, therefore imposing their own sense of quality above that of the authorised officer.

Analysing this content using a manifest approach where one reads the dialogue literally, it could be assumed that the member believes that planning and documentation for children should be relative to the moment rather than followed up through future planning. Investigating deeper into their thoughts and expressions, one can also see contention for the National Quality Standard, specifically the Assessment and Rating Process and the authorised officers' ability to view quality, therefore revealing their hidden agenda of potentially boycotting what the NQS possibly considers quality practice. This member serves to be strong in their discourse of what constitutes quality and uses many metaphorical phrases that cannot be taken literally. This latent data has the potential to be misconstrued yet highly influential in the field of beginning teachers with a strong emotionality behind the comments and potentially viewed as having an inflated ego.

In further analysis of this concept, particularly in relation to how this could influence the beginning teachers, there are clear messages for them as they emerge into their teaching practices. Firstly, learning is not based upon the activity provided, nor should it be followed up later than the moment the learning occurs. Further messages include some personal dogma that may influence beginning teachers to discard what the national legislation determines as quality practice and use their own discretion to determine what exactly is quality practice. The concepts clearly demonstrated in this example illustrate how personal opinion can receive more credit and influence than professional knowledge based upon sound research and empirical evidence.

Massey (2011) suggests that whilst manifest data can be used to establish how many times a particular theme or topic emerges, it is latent data that will give depth and meaning to the findings and therefore influence discussions and outcomes. He states "while manifest content may be extracted, the latent content will be the most relevant" (Massey, 2011, p. 24). He further suggests that manifest and latent data can be analysed at three approaches: grounded theory, phenomenology or thematic analysis. In this case, the dialogue is analysed using both a phenomenological approach and through thematic analysis.

3.3 Hot topics, sharing, emotionally driven expressions and unexpected phenomena

Coding: emerging themes in dialogue

Coding the discussions, similar to those mentioned, enabled me to establish key themes presently on the minds of both mentors and mentees that seemed to need frequent discussion and advice. I began to see patterns emerging of topics that attracted debate and argument, topics that required general advice and other topics that included a great deal of empathy and emotional support from their colleagues. The latter seemed to entail strong references to the mandated Assessment and Rating Process (where education and care services are assessed in their quality performance against national standards as well as legislative compliance), the role and expertise of authorised officers, lack of time and recognition for their work and workplace bullying. This was also the case between mentors in which general dialogue appeared more frequently, rather than targeted discourse between mentors and beginning teachers. These debates are explored in detail in the discussions chapter where I also combine elements of Heidegger's concepts of Being including the constructs of de-situation, intentionality and destabilisation.

Hot topics as defined by this research are the discussions that attracted debate and argument, with often two to five key members contributing and sometimes entering into what appears to be unprofessional discourse and even including personal attacks. Hot topics often began with a disclaimer pleading with members to refrain from mocking or abuse, but were clearly after some guidance and professional opinion relating to a topic of a seemingly controversial nature. The controversy, however, remains within the context of the early childhood sector as some topics, should they be removed from this pedagogical stance and shifted to another industry, may not be considered controversial at all. A strong example of this is the heated argument that began as a simple request for opinion upon artistic approaches and ended up with several personal attacks on several members within the discussion. Should this have been posted in perhaps another group designed for arts and crafts without the element of early childhood pedagogy, one might consider that there was no element of controversy presented in the original post. The hot topics have been coded into themes and sub-themes.

Creative expression

- What constitutes art in early childhood?

Planning and documentation

- Should planning and documentation be measured by the learning outcomes?

Cultural intelligence

- Should children be made to complete set craft activities for Christmas, Mother's Day and Father's Day, etc?
- Should you use real food in play?

Emotional wellbeing of children

- Should child performances such as concerts and graduation ceremonies be conducted with expectations placed upon children to participate?
- Should children with additional needs be excluded from services if you do not have the additional support?

Dialogue that focussed around sharing knowledge, ideas, thoughts and opinions generally maintained amicable decorum, although at times comments tended to leave the professional behaviour at bay, which meant that professional discussions varied and swayed between formal style posts and casual comments. These topics have been coded as follows:

Planning and documentation

- How do you document your planning and show clearly the planning cycle?
- What is critical reflection?
- How do you plan for babies and toddlers?

Working with others

- How do you get staff on board with your philosophy and ideals?
- How do you deal with difficult tertiary students on placement?

Understanding obligations

- Regulatory advice
- Industrial questions
- Seeking professional mentoring

Finally, dialogue that seemed to be emotionally driven as part of the teachers' frustrations with their profession, circumstances or political climate generally attracted the sharing of similar stories, empathy and words of comfort to each other, both between mentors and beginning teachers as well as mentors towards their peers. Specific topics of discussion have been coded as follows:

Help with obligations

- Expressions of stress and concern over the Assessment and Rating Process (including contention towards the delivery of the process specifically relating to the skills of the authorised officers)
- Expressions of feeling overworked, underpaid and not recognised in the sector and outside of the sector
- Frustrations at feeling time-poor with higher expectations on role performance yet provided with little time to achieve additional expectations

Wellbeing of educators

- Being unable to 'switch off' from work
- The value of Facebook networking
- Feelings of inadequacy and a loss of self-efficacy.

Coding: emerging nature of dialogue

Once the themes were coded in terms of topical themes, they were then placed into categories of helpful mentoring, condescending or conflicted mentoring and unexpected phenomena. This allowed for similar themes that emerged as a hot topic or a request for help to be categorised more rationally in relation to the research question, specifically focussing upon the impact Facebook is having upon beginning teachers. This supported the importance of understanding the nature of mentoring that was occurring rather than focussing exclusively upon the analysis of a theme or topic. In this case, the theme significant to this research then becomes the nature of mentoring and its potential impact upon the beginning teacher.

3.4 Helpful mentoring

Mentoring through Facebook was often seen to be helpful to others as a means of instant support and demonstration of professional behaviour. This was particularly evident for those seeking advice regarding industrial action and awards, which is a current concern in the Victorian sector at present, as well as guidance in preparation for the service's Assessment and Rating Visit by authorised officers. In this case Eller, Lev, and Feurer (2014) claim that good mentoring relationships exist with open and transparent communication that encumbers guidance in a variety of professional issues as well as support for beginning teachers as they transition to their new role or position of employment. A strong example of this comes from a beginning teacher requesting advice regarding children's hand preference and whether to promote one hand over the other. Responses for this beginning teacher varied with advice as well as information, although it is yet to be determined the validity or empirical evidence behind the advice. Such examples included mentors encouraging the beginning teacher to not be too concerned with hand preference at this stage, but to let it naturally develop, whilst other mentors stated that children now were struggling to develop pencil grips due to the amount of time they spent using devices. Whilst the initial responses were helpful, they were not determined to be accurate. A later response came making reference to Arnold Gesell, a medical pioneer in child development, and details regarding fine motor maturation and what to expect, including a reference, and despite this reference being sourced from 1947, it was a unique attempt at mentoring with research in mind. This also included acknowledgement from the beginning teacher to the mentor and how their contribution had been helpful.

Another example of helpful mentoring included a discussion regarding the tasks and activities when starting a new employment position and how to go about them. This question from a beginning teacher was specific in asking advice relating to establishing relationships and resources and texts that might be helpful for this time. In return, some lengthy and specific responses were posted from six educators who identified themselves as mentors to the group and included a piece of advice for the beginning teacher to sift back through previous discussions in the group that addressed these very issues. This approach could be interpreted in two different perspectives with one being that the mentor may have been tired with answering the same question, or they may have been trying to empower a new graduate to be proactive and vigilant in seeking specific information by developing their own research skills and resourcefulness. Other responses were more specific that included practical ideas for building relationships with children and families such as 'get to know you' forms, engaging in warm interactions with both children and families and remaining approachable. Other tips included exploring floor plans for the arrangement of the learning environment, developing contact lists and discussing with co-educators observations of children's play preferences and emerging friendships.

Helpful mentoring also took place in many other forms where beginning teachers sought the advice for complex issues that they felt they were not prepared for or adequately trained in addressing. Discussing complex issues in an open forum can attract both negative and positive responses; however Ellison, Gray, Lampe, and Fiore (2014) state in their exploration relating to Facebook and social capital that the manner in which the response is accepted or valued can vary according to the ties between the member who posts and the responder. This could also be the case for multiple respondents, their social ties to each other and to the original member. Examples of complex or controversial issues that were discussed resolving in helpful mentoring as stated by the original member posting included a discussion relating to end-of-year concerts in kindergarten. A beginning teacher was excited about how their first concert went feeling that this was successful and well enjoyed by both children and families. Responses to this post from group members were positive and warming to the beginning teacher. Interestingly though, a mentor did raise the aspect that concerts in early childhood can sometimes raise concerns in early childhood Facebook members as it is often seen as a contentious issue to bring up. This comment was followed on by applauding respondents for being encouraging rather than condescending.

Another question from a beginning teacher asked mentors ways in which they critically reflected as they were confused due to many opinions raised and debated. The responses to this question remained in positive viewpoint despite the potential to merge into argument regarding the word *critical*. The respondents provided ways in which they used critical reflection as well as encouraging others to see the word 'critical' as an analysing component rather than seeing practice with a negative lens. In fact, some respondents went into great detail about how they critically reflect upon their practice and how helpful it is in terms of improving what they do and how they perceive things. A further example of complex helpful mentoring was a thread that was a initiated by a member who had been contemplating the concept of children's *agency* and the comparable issues for children in Australia as opposed to children suffering poverty where survival and health becomes of more importance than agency. They also wanted to discuss the concept of agency in terms of whether a child's individual agency becoming more important than the group collective and what this meant in terms of democracy and respect. 'Agency' is a term used frequently in the EYLF and the NQS and has been a relatively new focus point for educators in early childhood resonating with the contemporary theories that are now included in early childhood education to promote aspects of social justice and shifting the power between adults and children (Kilderry, Nolan, & Scott, 2017). Agency relates to the child's ability to make decisions for themselves and on things that matter to them which is strongly incorporated into the learning outcomes for children as well as the opportunities educators should provide in relation to Quality Area one of the National Quality Standard (ACECQA, 2017).

This provocative post inspired many comments from others acting as mentors on this particular site and the discussion of agency in relation to children living in underdeveloped countries was contemplated and explored in various ways. This particular thread also illustrated the nature of mentors in how they would respond to such provocations with some stating that they would need to think about the concept first before they responded, whilst others were more reactive in their approach and applied the concept of agency to their own lifestyle rather than explore the construct as was given in its original context. Of particular interest in this discussion was the deliberation of 'agency' versus 'free will' with deeper thinking emerging from some of the mentors, exposing a higher level of contemplation in practice and understanding to the beginning teachers. Other, more randomly expressed comments did not hold such resonance and appeared to trivialise the original post where the member made comments about their own 'agency' on the weekend that illustrated aspects of cleaning, reading, writing and watching television. Their engagement with the topic by trivialising 'agency' had the potential to create dissonance amongst members, however was mostly ignored.

As we can see, the very nature in engagement with the network varies according to the nature of the post as well as the virtual identity of the respondent. These examples, despite some trivialisation of topics, still tend to remain as a positive influence for beginning teachers as they explored theoretical, philosophical and practical aspects of their profession, possibly leading to increased sense of self-efficacy. However, despite the many positive and enriching threads and conversations, the darker side of the profession has also revealed itself with some members utilising their detached, virtual persona to not only engage in online arguments, but also in condescending behaviours to both mentor colleagues and mentees.

3.5 Condescending and conflicting mentoring

In searching for further threads of helpful hints, supports and guidance, it became apparent that this was not the only type of engagement that took place in the arena of social media. In fact, threads that caught my eye demonstrated that some members felt it necessary to forewarn others in anticipation of possible public ill-treatment and therefore would begin their post pleading with potential responders to not abuse or post anything insulting in return, in which case was at times ignored. This practice could imply that either they have experienced condescending responses prior, they have themselves given a condescending response or they have witnessed these types of responses towards others. A clear example of this was a heated debate that emerged on an educational leaders' early childhood forum during a discussion regarding what constitutes art for the toddler room. The original post came from a member pleading with potential responders to not shame or abuse them in their questioning indicating anticipated ill-treatment where the member went to lengths of warning, pre-empting a possible attack. To explain the context of the thread and its potential controversial nature, a photograph of a child's 'art' was posted with a question asking for colleagues to provide advice as to whether a footprint of the toddler with added accessories such as eyes, legs, wings, etc drawn by the educator constituted the work of the toddler's art. Not only did this provoke philosophical and pedagogical debate upon what is considered true art for a toddler, but also included emotionally charged attacks and defence responses, deviating from the question in hand and quest for advice. Whilst the discussion involved many comments relating to what educators believed to be art, it also delved harshly into a personal arena of referring to the educator's intention as being *egotistical* and *self-gratifying*. Other educators demonstrated deep anger in relation to this type of artwork occurring in early childhood education, whilst others challenged this passionate opposition and commented that there may be a time and place for such things. The challenges of pedagogical lenses proceeded to then spark personal responses that led to a path of unprofessional and potentially unethical behaviour from early childhood mentoring educators in a public forum. Tensions gained further velocity as the discussion continued and targeted specific members, including myself where I had commented (as researcher as participant) that perhaps this was focussed more about the process of relational engagement between the educator and the child rather than bringing about creative art. To this, a member promptly replied that I had missed the point and continued to denigrate my own thoughts and opinions of the conversation. The personal attacks did not stop there as two other members of the thread began to argue in reciprocity regarding the intentionality behind their comments and whether or not they had direct intention to insult or belittle each other and began blaming each other for initiating insults. It is at this point that the thread began to lose momentum of the original content with the discussion of art integrity becoming of least importance and the discussion of insult and blame becoming the focus. Finally, the debate ended with a controversial statement from one of the members who claimed that scrutinising each other's opinions was in fact healthy, rather than all agreeing, as it provided room for professional growth. However, it seemed that other members of this thread may not have agreed as they did not comment any further and in fact the original member who asked the question left the early childhood forum group altogether.

This particular early childhood forum was aimed at providing networking between educational leaders and therefore posts and comments could be perceived as role-modelling to others; possibly even role-modelling to the leaders of beginning teachers or beginning teachers themselves. The nature of role-modelling according to this thread may therefore be seen as acceptable to openly and disrespectfully critique and 'scrutinise' the professional opinions of others, rather than having a professional debate of such topics. Eller et al. (2014) describe effective mentoring strategies to include good communication and collegiality with those whom they are mentoring, ensuring that wisdom is shared through planned activities. Eller et al. (2014) also refer to mentoring having two functions: one being psychosocial whereby the mentee's sense of self-efficacy, professional identity and self-worth is preserved and enhanced whilst career functions are also highlighted, protecting and challenging the mentee as they grow and learn professionally. The particular thread seems to provoke underlying tones of dissonance and discursive conversations which in fact seemed to attack the self-efficacy of members who had posted comments and whilst opinions were challenged, mentees were not protected.

This form of informal mentoring on a variety of discussion groups is concerning as beginning teachers are also members of such groups, given that their qualification may have lifted their career progression to educational leader within their work environment, despite recently graduating as a degree-trained teacher. It cannot be confirmed that all members of the leadership groups were in fact bachelor-trained staff and after some investigation into the identity of some members, it become clear that some members were not only untrained, but did not have a leadership role in their professional workplace at all. This brings to question the decision-making process in membership of such groups and where the intent is for a group to gather as educational leaders, yet the membership only exists as virtual educational leadership. What does this mean for the sector? Who is leading who and with what training in leadership and level of experience comes with that?

Revisiting these sites in 2016 in anticipation for further resolution and increased professional behaviour, disappointment was realised as on a similar site for educational leaders, a more serious and vindictive thread was posted; this time in response to a previous post that caused significant stir among the early childhood leadership sector.

An altercation had occurred publicly between a member and an administrator of the group where the member was demonstrating some concern about the validity of some of the registered training organisations that were 'passing' students even if they did not demonstrate competence. The member was then warned to reflect upon her opinions which then spiralled quickly into a heated debate where the administrator finally deleted altogether the thread of discussion initiated by the member. Seemingly furious, the member then created a new post, whilst almost poetic in nature, was directly aimed at an administrator of the group for being hypocritical in deleting the thread and claiming that the act was unfair and an abuse of power. As the discussion continued, it became apparent that according to members of the group, the administrator whom the member was attacking also frequently vocalises much of their philosophical viewpoint with somewhat ignorance to the possible dissonance or offensiveness it may cause to others, yet allegedly expected a more dignified approach from other members themselves when posting on 'their' forum. The administrator's response, however, continued to argue or justify their position and argued that when they typically 'rant' it is usually about 'bad practice' and even though they admitted that this came back to *their perception* of bad practice, they boldly commented that usually they were right.

The conversation appeared to escalate in what then became the battle of *what you said* and *what I meant* becoming a literal struggle between latent and manifest meaning, personal attacks without revocation and an inability to resolve without more senior members other than the administrator themselves stepping in to take the conversation to a more fruitful path. Furthermore, this particular early childhood forum strongly believed in ensuring that all threads remained available for viewing and as part of its philosophy all comments were valued as part of the context of the thread which was in contrast to the administrator's act of removing the member's thread. In response to such philosophy some members left this particular group leaving powerful statements of disappointment at the degradation that was occurring between members and between members and the administrator.

Aside from arguments and bouts of unethical and unprofessional conduct from educators in the field, there was also an element of conflicting mentoring. This type of mentoring took the form of multiple responses from mentors to a single post whereby a single answer would suffice yet varying answers provided. Conflicting mentoring also existed across sites whereby the same question was asked by a mentee yet different answers provided, therefore confusing the beginning teacher rather than supporting them. For example, on several early childhood forums a question was asked relating to the inclusion of religion in curriculum, particularly in relation to Christmas and the belief of Santa as well as religious Christmas crafts. On some forums mentors responded with complex situations that can occur when Santa is or is not included in curriculum. For example, one member spoke of a child who did not practice the belief in Santa who then continued to 'spoil' this for other children who did, advising that by engaging with parents to discuss the 'issue,' it helped to keep the 'magic.' Meanwhile, others explicitly stated that the educator should explain that Santa only comes to deliver presents to the house of those who believe in him. On another site, a similar topic was introduced with mentors responding with comments that encouraged educators to divert the topic of Santa and his 'realness' to the family to address and not the responsibility of the educator. This is an example of varied practice, but all with the intention of advising the original member what to do in relation to the belief of 'Santa' in the early childhood curriculum.

3.6 Unexpected phenomena

A key phenomenon emerged through some sites aimed at supporting beginning teachers that was significant enough to draw attention to as an emerging additional form of research investigation. It became apparent that many of the experienced teachers' posts who were acting as mentors to beginning teachers were also seeking mentoring from others on the same Facebook forum. This phenomenon was particularly strong in a page designed specifically for beginning teachers and it appeared irrelevant that this page was explicitly aimed to support teachers who were in their first or second year of teaching, or those who were about to graduate. Some comments from the mentors included the expression of feelings of inadequacy, frustrations, feeling unappreciated or general pleas for advice and support. As these posts were visible to the mentees (beginning teachers), this forum for mentoring demonstrated possibilities that the mentors offering mentorship to the beginning teachers may be experiencing a lack of confidence in their own roles and sense of efficacy. This poses a potential concern that perhaps some teachers acting as mentors may not be adequately qualified or experienced enough in their leadership and mentoring practices to be mentoring others. This could be due to a lack in leadership and mentoring training, or exposure to good mentoring when they were previously mentees. For example, a question was asked of beginning teachers how they felt about their first year in teaching in which both mentors and mentees described how they were struggling, experiencing stress and depression, questioning their efficacy in their profession and that they were extremely time-poor.

Some of the statements were particularly concerning to the current climate of the early childhood sector in Australia and not only how the reforms are impacting upon beginning teachers, but also experienced teachers who are relied upon for their mentorship. Hallam, Chou, Hite, and Hite (2012) discuss the effects of good mentoring with reference to both the professional relationship and the personal relationship. They suggest that there needs to be an element of trust and friendship between the beginning teacher and the mentor with the latter strongly modeling life-long learning to the mentee. "Successful mentoring includes effective modeling and support. Good mentoring provides guidance and facilitates the socialization of beginning teachers" (p. 246). This presents some possible adversities in the concepts of dialogue between mentors and their arising sense of vulnerability in their own workplace, and has the potential to role-model mentoring inadequacies. On the other hand, it can also serve to bring empathy to the beginning teacher enlightening them that mentors at times struggle as well and lean towards networking support from their peers to get them through the day-to-day business of work-life obstacles. Mentoring in this sense becomes more about the co-construction of learning in partnership, rather than the novice/expert relationship.

Discussions about mentoring

In addition to the previous discussions, another interesting topic that emerged frequently was the request for information regarding funded formal mentoring programs. Discussions revolved around members' involvement in previous programs and if anyone knew of new programs that may be on offer. Responses included referring to the mentoring project offered through Victoria University and Deakin University; however advice included that whilst the project was successful, it had now ceased with inferences made to governmental funding cuts. Interestingly, one beginning teacher asked the question exactly how to find a mentor to which there was no reply. Various reasons could be for this including members moving on to other threads for discussion or simply not really knowing what they were actually looking for in terms of mentorship. In another thread, a mentor member responded to a beginning teacher who was introducing themselves to the forum with advice in why it is important to find a mentor as soon as possible and how beneficial this was for them when they had graduated. This comment highlights the benefits that mentoring could play in the life of a beginning teacher based upon a mentor's previous experience which brings to the forefront the value of effective mentoring. What is possibly lacking here is advice in what to look for in a mentor and for the teacher to think about what it is exactly they would like to receive from being a part of a mentoring partnership.

Unresponsive mentoring versus mentoring in abstract thinking

A further interesting phenomena that emerged was at times the lack of response from mentors to beginning teachers and sometimes minimal advice to seemingly important questions to the life of the beginning teacher as they begin to explore the working environment. For example, some members posted their availability for work or sought advice in how to improve their English skills to gain further employment to which there was no reply. The lack of response is interesting to note here and also contemplating the reasoning behind the lack of response as well as what messages it could be unintentionally giving to those who posted these questions. Once again it could be due to monitoring issues on behalf of the administrators, or that the focus of this group is not necessarily to help new graduates find work, but to explore pedagogy and contemporary issues. Ellison et al. (2014) describe the motivations for response to be gratifying both for the member who posted originally, and also the responders which could indicate as to why some posts have more responses than others. Incorporating the construct of social capital in terms of Facebook connections, they also argue that networks can be seen as investments in relationships and therefore the more intricate the response, the more one invests in the relationship (Ellison et al., 2014). A particular example post and subsequent thread clearly illustrates this where a discussion took place between mentors regarding the concept of gender and the identity of teacher. The initial post utilised a quote from a fantasy writer who explored the influence of gender as main characters in books. The mentor posting this quote included challenging the idea that her identity as a 'teacher', whilst it did not solely define her, was not as obvious to others; however gender explicitly defined her as it was evident to others that she was a 'woman.' The conversation that followed, whilst it did not include beginning teachers, introduced contributors to the forum, aspects of abstract thinking that could build the investment of the network in terms of social capital and the early childhood teaching community. This brings in a more intricate picture of the nature of helpful mentoring that is occurring on Facebook as new beginning teachers begin to be exposed not just to possible short or long answers to their posts for practical help, but to also see the deeper critical thinking that may occur in terms of a teacher's understanding of their identity and place within the teaching paradigm.

Rants about theory and practice

A final unexpected phenomenon that seemed to emerge in the Facebook forums was the need to *rant*. Ranting took place in various forms, including dissatisfaction with workplace conditions, colleagues and policies, as well as families classified as difficult and unreasonable. Of particular interest, though was observing that the ranting often did not necessarily take place in relation to theory and how this could or could not be applied to early childhood practices. As I sifted through many of the posts and threads, theory was not entirely evident in many of the discussions held between educators, which causes deliberation to be further discussed in the next chapter. Rants, however seemed to regularly take the form of dogma from the individual members. For example, one member articulated their frustrations at other co-workers who were putting in above and beyond personal time to their job which inadvertently impacted upon those who valued their family life and could not devote such time and were therefore seen as potentially 'less-devoted' to teaching because of this. Other members ranted in relation to their frustrations that some parents would not take their advice for their child to have a second year of kindergarten, despite the time, effort and opinion of the teacher. The responses to this post varied in nature as well as length and advice, however seemed to hold the same sentiment of the rant in relation to children having a second year of funded preschool. For instance, one respondent replied that they could understand the pain the 'ranter' was going through, whilst others simply stated they had similar experiences with preparing a second-year application only to learn at the last minute that a child had gone on to school. An interesting response was that of a teacher who was also a parent and in the process of deciding whether or not to have their own child complete a second year of funded preschool. This then changed the main theme of the discussion as respondents began to encourage and support this member in 'doing the right thing' by making the child repeat. Whilst the intention behind this may have been genuine, remnants of dogmatic ranting and coercion can be seen in the discussion as multiple members joined the argument to convince the teacher/parent they were making the right decision.

The following chapter will now explore what this means in terms of the possible impact these types of engagements may be having on beginning teachers. Using literature these arguments will highlight the positive and negative aspects of engagement of Facebook and what this also may mean for the professional identity of the early childhood teaching profession.

References

Australian Children's Education and Care Quality Authority (ACECQA). (2017). *Guide to the national quality framework*. Sydney: Australian Children's Education and Care Quality Authority.

Barbour, R. S., & Schostak, J. (2011). Interviewing and focus groups. In B. Somekh & C. Lewin (Eds.), *Theory and methods in social research*. 2nd ed., pp. 61–67. London: SAGE Publications Ltd. (Reprinted from: 2006).

Eller, L. S., Lev, E. L., & Feurer, A. (2014). Key components of an effective mentoring relationship: A qualitative study. *Nurse Education Today*, *34*(5), 815–820. doi:10.1016/j.nedt.2013.07.020

Ellison, N. B., Gray, R., Lampe, C., & Fiore, A. T. (2014). Social capital and resource requests on Facebook. *New Media & Society*, *16*(7), 1104–1121. doi:10.1177/1461444814543998

Gray, D. E. (2014). *Doing research in the real world*. 3rd ed. Los Angeles, CA: SAGE.

Hallam, P. R., Chou, P. N., Hite, J. M., & Hite, S. J. (2012). Two contrasting models for mentoring as they affect retention of beginning teachers. *National Association of Secondary School Principals. NASSP Bulletin*, *96*(3), 243–278.

Kilderry, A., Nolan, A., & Scott, C. (2017). 'Out of the loop': Early childhood educators gaining confidence with unfamiliar policy discourse. *Early Years*, *37*(4), 341–354. doi:10.1080/09575146.2016.1183595

Massey, O. T. (2011). A proposed model for the analysis and interpretation of focus groups in evaluation research. *Evaluation and Program Planning*, *34*(1), 21–28. doi:10.1016/j.evalprogplan.2010.06.003

Smith, J. A., Flowers, P., & Larkin, M. (2009). *Interpretive Phenomenological Analysis: Theory, Method and Research*. London: SAGE Publications Ltd.

4 Implications for future EC teachers

This chapter will bring together the findings and the literature and directly conclude at this stage of the research project the directions that mentoring seems to be taking in terms of Facebook and the influence this may be having upon our future teachers and beginning teachers. It will relate back to the issues discussed in the introduction and also provide any suggestions of the pathways that may need to be taken to address the issue further and also deepen the research with additional investigations.

4.1 Facebook culture in the early childhood sector

The early childhood sector has readily embraced Facebook as a means of networking, sharing knowledge and essentially mentoring. From the findings we can see that there are many educators taking a strong and active role both in mentoring experienced educators as well as targeting support for beginning teachers. In the work of Ellison, Gray, Lampe, and Fiore (2014) the call for help gratifies both the asker and the respondent and they further discuss the gratifying nature of Facebook in terms of building social capital and enhancing knowledge base through this medium. The early childhood Facebook culture demonstrates this clearly as there are many calls for help and advice across many sites, whilst also a large avenue for 'rants.' The nature of 'ranting' on Facebook is literal in terms that early childhood Facebook members also refer to themselves as 'ranting' or 'having a rant.' To define the concept of 'ranting' we refer to the works of Graham Francis Badley who so eloquently and poetically defined ranting as "a turgid declamation, a tirade, a piece of bombast, a scolding, a violent storming" (Badley, 2015, p. 759). Badley (2015) explores the very nature of ranting in qualitative context particularly in relation to radicalisation and social change. He further explores the possible purposes of ranting including being able to be heard by those who normally only listen to and act upon academic rhetoric without the inclusion of listeners who understand language outside of this circle (Badley, 2015). What Badley was trying to articulate was that qualitative research can in fact be written in the form of a rant in order for the research to reach those who can enact the recommendations of the research through understanding and relating to the ranting. Ranting, therefore according to Badley appears to be a perfectly reasonable way to express not only opinions, but findings and conclusions with the anticipation that these recommendations will in fact take place, although not necessarily in the format of radicalisation but perhaps mindset change. This incites possible pedagogical shifts and change brought about by the research which is strongly evident in the threads posted on the early childhood Facebook sites. When we refer to the thread relating to a member's attitude towards the assessment and rating process we see that this member perhaps has a strong stance against the ability to measure quality due to such variances of perception of authorised officers. Ranting is clearly seen in the example where a member articulated their frustrations with parents changing their mind about their child having a second year of funded preschool, or the anonymous member who felt perplexed that their colleagues felt perfectly happy to devote extra personal time to their working life in order to improve their quality.

In observance of general Facebook threads, it also becomes apparent that 'ranting' has possibly become a freely and frequently chosen medium for expressing one's opinion without restraint. In fact, early childhood is not unique to the practice of 'ranting' on Facebook. Ranting is a common phenomenon on Facebook and has also seen to be challenged in court such as the case of Thomas Smith who was sentenced for 'ranting' against the U.S. police through unlawful use of communication media which was later overturned under the protection of the US constitutional First Amendment ("Appeals judge rules Facebook rant protected by First Amendment (UPDATE)," 2014). A further example of a rant ending up in court was that of a 14-year-old student in Oregon, USA who used violent referrals to his health teacher. This also ended with the judge declaring that the student did not pose any real threat, as well as the support of the community also stating he had the right to his freedom of speech (Walsh, 2015). Whilst this could bring us to a deeper level of discussion regarding the construct of freedom of speech and its relationship with Facebook, as addressed and challenged by a member challenging an administrator in their power over others to voice their opinions, as described in the previous chapter, it is important to begin to form a picture in how the use of Facebook including the ranting, advice and networking can impact upon the beginning early childhood teacher, particularly in relation to their professional identity and self-efficacy, confidence in practice and understanding of early childhood pedagogical contexts, not to mention ideas around professional and ethical conduct.

4.2 Destabilisation in the virtual world of mentoring

Beginning teachers are particularly vulnerable in their first years in the workforce and as previously mentioned, account for a large number of leavers in the profession due to burnout, dissatisfaction and disillusionment (Macfarlane & Noble, 2005; O'Neill & Stephenson, 2012). In addition, the early childhood sector in Australia has historically found difficulty in sustaining a strong professional identity as well as effective leadership that could influence a higher level of thinking and professional code of conduct, all contributing to the professional efficacy of the sector (Fenech, 2013; Stamopoulos, 2012). This is now possibly destabilised further by the behaviours observed through Facebook threads and the question can now be asked, is Facebook de-professionalising the early childhood profession, including their next generation of teachers? Upon reading the aforementioned posts and rants, one could quite clearly answer 'yes'; however we must tread cautiously before committing to that conclusion as we can see that Facebook certainly also provides an avenue of support and networking which at times can bring great relief to those who are experiencing some isolation in the field, whether it be professional or physical isolation.

According to Crowell (2013) and his interpretation of Heidegger's sense of Being or the nature of *Dasein* (being there) one could consider that Facebook is providing an avenue of 'being there' without actually 'being there.' Our professional identities as mentors become destabilised as we strive to appear in one sense a professional, yet in our rants appear as another. We flee from our truth and yet reveal it in the same breath. We return once again to the concept of credibility behind the mask of mentor, educational leader, experienced teacher and the like and conjure an identity to appeal to the vulnerable and the needy, the beginning early childhood teachers. If we look closely to the heated conversation between the members in the leadership forum who were grappling with each other over whose right it was to utilise freedom of speech, we begin to see that there appears to be some sort of hidden permission as to the enabled and the disempowered that some members have over others and that identity and status within the group facilitates credibility to this. Whilst the administrator strongly argued that the previous comment made to the group member was not in any way debilitating their right to freedom of speech, this was not the actual perception of the member who then accused the administrator of being hypocritical and presumptuous and abusing their power as an administrator.

Here we can see that the group member challenged the credibility of leadership of the administrator and their freedom to speak without restraint, yet was denied that very freedom themselves to the point of withdrawing from the group altogether. The battles of power that emerge here are strongly linked to the aspect of identity in terms of the leader (administrator) as opposed to the follower (general group member) who has now resigned themselves to refrain from sharing their thoughts, or modelling their leadership and ideas to others (remembering that this group is devoted to membership of educational leaders). The comments from observers to this conversation interestingly validated the administrator's stance and access to freedom of speech in this particular argument which brings about the status of this role within the group which we could therefore identify the administrator as the 'leader.' Once again, we see here the element of intentionality where the administrator is the mentor as they are seen to be by others on the forum. Heidegger, as interpreted by Crowell (2013) might consider that a socialist approach has been taken here as opposed to an individualistic approach with not just one leader destabilising the profession, but many, as other members of the conversation supported the administrator's statements and dismissive approach to the disgruntled member's plea to be heard and understood. What we also see here is a moment in time of existence within the virtual world as opposed to the 'real world.' One therefore may question and ponder would there have been alternative consequences if this conversation had taken place in the exact same manner in the real world where humans are face-to-face and exposing themselves to confrontation, not virtually, but within the realms of realism? Could this be as previously mentioned by Grondin (2005, loc. 415) "an inauthentic form of existence?" Is it that these comments are made because we have the freedom to choose whether to look back on it or not and are not physically faced with the repercussions of the argument in our physical world? This also realigns with Ellison et al. (2014) and their argument that whilst comments from those we value may have more attention, comments from those we are less connected to may be more helpful. They further state "responses from weaker ties and stronger ties were equally satisfying, that is, people like and value signals of attention from their network, regardless of how well the responses address their expressed request" (Ellison et al., 2014, p. 1108). Here we also have evidence of this as the debate discussed was the second part (following on) from another thread that had previously been deleted due to the hostility that was arising between members. What we can see in this very conversation posted is that regardless of how we appear, how we are identified to others by our comments and whether others agree, it is the attention from the network that is mostly valued and therefore ultimately insatiable. As the conversation ended, there is wonder as to whether the administrator will continue on with their day considering that they had addressed what they needed to with a sense that they were supported by the members of their group in their comments and action. Meanwhile what of the disgruntled member and their deflated resignation to withdraw from comment and engagement? Did they leave the networking behind or take it with them into the place of work where they were yet to enact in reality their role of educational leadership to others? Would this member now feel disempowered in their actual role on the ground or could it stay de-situated in cyberspace?

The importance behind what we see in terms of the destabilisation of the profession is the manner in which it is impacting upon beginning teachers as they view their role-models engaged in behaviours that contradict the sector's fundamental code of ethics as guided by Early Childhood Australia (ECA). The ECA Code of Ethics holds educators with strong accountability in relation to their treatment of children, families, colleagues, students and the community as well as the treatment of themselves and was originally developed for the early childhood sector to "promote ethical practice and the development of professional status" (Jackiewicz, 2015, p. 34). The example we have just deeply discussed highlights the possibilities that the sector either is not aware of the national code of ethics, despite the National Quality Standard requiring educators to practice an ethical code of conduct, or they lack self-regulation in a public (and published) space due to the abstract engagement of Facebook and the ability to escape one's own truth in the virtual world. Referring back to the ECA Code of Ethics, it can be said that whilst Jackiewicz (2015) claims that "It is both a tool for advocacy and a framework for reflective practice" (p. 34), one questions how educators on Facebook are role-modelling its use and usefulness. What a beginning teacher might see here is an element of disrespect and disregard for their colleagues as well as a lack in reflexive practice, both strong elements that feature within the code. In saying this there were other examples they could refer to that were positive examples of respect and reflexivity which included a teacher's provocations relating to gender and agency and the positive group responses received or the member who offered a supportive response and advice to a beginning teacher relating to critical reflection; all complex and controversial issues, yet discussed with robust enthusiasm and allowance for differentiated opinions. It is this very nature of posting where beginning teachers seem to feel more comfortable to engage. This was highlighted also through another recent thread on a site targeted at supporting beginning teachers where the opinions of the members were sought as to the usefulness, approach and direction of the group. Responses to this reflexivity included many positive compliments congratulating the administrators for keeping a close eye on the potential arousal of negativity and working through any issues in a discreet and proactive manner. This brings us to the next concept to discuss, being the intentionality behind the engagement in mentorship through Facebook forums.

4.3 Intentionality: what are you doing here?

Reflecting back to Nolan and Rouse's (2013) findings that more and more double degree teachers are choosing the profession of primary teacher as opposed to early childhood sector, it has now come to the pointy end of the argument in addressing attrition and relating this to intentionality in the context of Heidegger. More than ever before bachelor-trained teachers are required by larger numbers in early childhood settings due to the new legislative requirements and quality standards. However, despite this need, the sector is losing beginning teachers to the primary school sector who, interestingly in Victoria, have had a formal mentoring program through their teacher registration processes for many years. The year 2016 was the first year the formal mentoring program was introduced to Victorian early childhood teachers due to the change in processes that early childhood teachers must now be registered with the Victorian Institute of Teaching (VIT). The *Effective Mentoring Program* is operated in partnership between DET and VIT with the anticipation that mentors will support beginning teachers through to full registration after a required number of years in teaching and provides guiding materials and workshops to support experienced teachers in effectively mentoring beginning teachers (Department of Education and Training, 2016). What is unique to the early childhood sector is that both the experienced teachers and beginning teachers are for the first time reflecting upon specific teaching standards which implicates that even the experienced teachers may need mentoring in how to apply the standards to their own teaching practice, let alone to that of a beginning teacher. What this program offers is an expectation both of experienced teachers (mentors) and beginning teachers (mentees) to come to a mutual understanding of how they will go about the mentorship and plan for it. The practice therefore of intentionality lies within the actions and practices of the mentor, as Heidegger would consider the 'third-person.' *I am a mentor because I am viewed as a mentor and my actions and practices illustrate that I am mentoring*. The Effective Mentoring Program requires mentors to attend workshop training and a report of the skills and achievements of the beginning teacher as they progress through the stages of full registration (Department of Education and Training, 2016).

Back-flipping to Facebook in comparison with this, the view of the mentor now does not necessarily take the shape of Heidegger's version of intentionality, but instead can be viewed through the eyes of the first-person. *I am the mentor because that is what is in my head; so I will start my own Facebook group and I will mentor the members*. The danger here is that there is no evidence of formal mentoring training nor leadership development bestowed upon the alleged mentor; instead they declare themselves as mentor with the intention to be seen by others as *mentor*. This practice was apparent for the administrator in the leadership group as they declared themselves a member through their privileged power on their Facebook forum with the support of the majority of their followings. How the beginning teacher views the nature of both types of mentoring, online and offline, is yet to be seen; however the most evidential piece of information that has come from this study is that beginning teachers may be more likely to be mentored when they feel the mentoring space is safe, respectful and well supported. This now brings us to conclusive statements that will lead to the next stages of the research project.

References

Appeals judge rules Facebook rant protected by First Amendment (UPDATE). (2014, 07/03). *Wisconsin Law Journal*.

Badley, G. F. (2015). Qualitative ranting? *Qualitative Inquiry*, *21*(9), 759–765. doi:10.1177/1077800415569791

Crowell, S. (2013). *Normativity and phenomenology in Husserl and Heidegger*. New York: Cambridge University Press.

Department of Education and Training (DET). (2016). A Reflective Guide to Mentoring and Being and Early Childhood Teacher-Mentor. Melbourne, Australia: State of Victoria (Department of Education and Training).

Ellison, N. B., Gray, R., Lampe, C., & Fiore, A. T. (2014). Social capital and resource requests on Facebook. *New Media & Society*, *16*(7), 1104–1121. doi:10.1177/1461444814543998

Fenech, S. (2013). Leadership development during times of reform. *Australasian Journal of Early Childhood*, *38*, 89+.

Grondin, J. (2005). Why reawaken the question of being? In R. Polt (Ed.), *Heidegger's Being and Time: Critical Essays*. Maryland, USA: Rowman and Littlefield Publishers, Inc.

Jackiewicz, S. (2015). Reviewing the code of ethics [online]. *Every Child*, *21*(1), 34–35.

Macfarlane, K., & Noble, K. (2005). Romance or reality? Examining burnout in early childhood teachers. *Australian Journal of Early Childhood*, *30*, 53+.

Nolan, A., & Rouse, E. (2013). Where to from here? Career choices of pre-service teachers undertaking a dual early childhood/primary qualification [online]. *Australian Journal of Teacher Education (Online)*, *38*(1), 1–10.

O'Neill, S., & Stephenson, J. (2012). Exploring Australian pre-service teachers sense of efficacy, its sources, and some possible influences. *Teaching and Teacher Education*, *28*(4), 535–545. doi:10.1016/j.tate.2012.01.008

Stamopoulos, E. (2012). Reframing early childhood leadership. *Australasian Journal of Early Childhood*, *37*, 42+.

Walsh, M. (2015, 13 May). Student's Facebook Rant Ruled Free Speech. *Education Week*, *34*, 4.

5 Future impact

5.1 Conclusive statements and recommendations

The equation of beginning teachers, mentoring and Facebook leaves us with an answer that is forever changing and is currently unstill and in fact, spurs us to have more questions. What we do know is that many early childhood practitioners, whether they be trained or untrained, like to engage and network through social media, particularly Facebook. They share photographs of learning environments, documentation templates and children's artwork as well as engage in voracious discussions relating to social justice, children's rights and pedagogy. We also know that early childhood practitioners, and not just teachers alone, bring with them a culture of Facebook usage that is of daily, if not hourly practice for some and that the instant and continual connectivity means that the dialogue is never-ending. Once one conversation ends, another begins. Educators appear to be always thinking, always wanting to know more and always wanting to check in with each other about this knowledge. This means that the culture of activity on Facebook is not only impacting upon the practices that we implement with children, but also the inner thoughts of the early childhood practitioner about their practice, their knowledge and their efficacy as a teacher. This endless dialogue does not just exist within the workplace, but enters into the life of the educator at home, but perhaps also when they are out to dinner, attending a conference, at their child's sports day or even during a traditional celebration such as Easter or Christmas. Being a member of an early childhood Facebook forum does not necessarily allow for educators to 'switch off' at the end of the day particularly if it is at this time that Facebook is checked, either for personal or professional reasons. This illustrates a significant impact engagement on Facebook is having for all participants which may add another layer to educator 'burnout.' This is particularly concerning for beginning teachers as 'burnout' is a common risk factor for the first few years of teaching and therefore withdrawal from the profession altogether (Tankersley, 2010).

On a superficial level, or at least that which is exposed through this endless dialogue on Facebook, there seems to be both positive and negative elements to the engagement. For one, there is demonstration of some level of leadership provided for the mentee through the act of asking for and receiving advice and guidance based upon experience. This is important for the beginning teacher, particularly if they find themselves working in a setting where effective leadership and pedagogical guidance is minimal or from a manager or leader who is not appropriately trained in this field (Fenech, 2013). There are also opportunities for beginning teachers to learn how to professionally engage in hot topic discussions by observing both professional and unprofessional behaviours on Facebook and any 'call to action' in relation to ethical challenges from members when the conversation begins to decline. Opportunities for posting practical questions also support the progress of development in both the beginning teacher and the mentor particularly around engagement with families, documentation processes and even funding applications. The concerning factors that arise from this however, include the possibility that Facebook may replace some rigorous and highly regarded professional development, coaching and mentoring opportunities that are formed from evidence-based research. Programs such as the Effective Mentoring Program may not necessarily be taken up so diligently if beginning teachers feel that engagement on Facebook has a more instant and reliable response rate.

Facebook also is the platform for mixed-messages where contradicting advice may confound the reader, impacting upon the practicalities of implementing aspects of this advice. This means that the beginning teacher has to make professional decisions upon which piece of advice they will apply without certainty of knowing that the advice is based upon evidence or context. For example, mentors may advise upon the use of electronic platforms for documenting children's learning and development so that they can be shared with families, however this may mean very little to the beginning teacher's community that may not have reliable internet or access to unlimited data storage.

Is Facebook just a platform for ranting?

Our discussions relating to ranting have the potential to influence the beginning teacher strongly in that it may inadvertently promote Facebook as a place for a 'rant' with the variances of ranting ranging from possibly prejudiced and discriminatory rants (such as excluding children with additional needs from their services) to rants of activism (such as unhappiness with industrial awards that include protests and stopwork actions as well as attacks on politicians). However, Badley (2015) discusses that 'ranting' is not necessarily a negative attribute of Facebook as it can effect social change that is perhaps necessary in some instances, teaching the beginning teacher that speaking up for the rights of children, families and teachers is important as part of a progressive society. Therefore, whilst it might be a platform for ranting, this nature of engagement serves multiple purposes such as instant gratification of being free to 'have a rant,' as discussed in the next section, the opportunity for comfort and support from colleagues as well as moments where the concepts behind the rant may be professionally addressed in terms of social justice. It is the manner in which ranting itself is conducted and responded to that impacts upon the development of professionalism in the beginning teacher's mind over time and therefore possibly impact upon the way they too conduct their own 'ranting' on- and offline.

Is it about gratification?

It is understandable that beginning teachers turn to Facebook in the absence of effective face-to-face mentoring, given that this platform is often instant and accessible. Does this mean that our culture of new teachers relies then upon the instant gratification of receiving an answer to their question through Facebook, rather than using their own problem-solving skills to work through situations in their workplace? Whilst social capital and the knowledge base of teaching and pedagogy builds through Facebook as discussed by Ellison, Gray, Lampe, and Fiore (2014), consideration to the development of the professional skills of the beginning teacher must be taken. Should instant advice be always accessible, we run the risk of beginning teachers building a reliance upon the instant gratification of advice receiving rather than full engagement in reflective practice. It is therefore imperative that the level of instant gratification be considered when providing advice to beginning teachers on Facebook and the way in which it is delivered so that it supports the teacher to become more reflective rather than predominantly receptive. The use of open-ended questions, concepts to consider and possibilities may need to be the first point of call, rather than giving the answer immediately. This draws back to the important issue discussed earlier regarding the level of leadership and mentoring training that mentors may or may not have when they are engaging on Facebook and acting in the mentor role. Training in online mentoring, particularly SNS such as Facebook, may need to be further considered in future leadership programs such as those offered at the Bastow Institute of Educational Leadership.

Is the intentionality behind mentoring authentic?

We once again bring ourselves to the argument of intentionality and the motivation behind the mentor and their engagement in mentoring on

Facebook. Advice giving and advice receiving can be obscured through the intentionality of the mentor and mentee in terms of the hidden agendas behind both. We ponder if the mentor sees themselves as a mentor because they act like one on Facebook, but is this the case in reality? With the multiple (including fake) Facebook profiles, avatars or pseudonyms used to disguise who they really are, we begin to question this intentionality behind their mentoring. Is it that they genuinely seek to help others, or is there an ulterior motive to convince the beginning teacher of the values and beliefs of the mentor and therefore follow in their footsteps of professional practice and pedagogy? Understanding that intentionality, as described by Crowell (2013) in his interpretation of Heidegger's philosophy, is subjective to our own thoughts and what we wish to reveal about ourselves; there is an element of authenticity that can be questioned here. There must also be consideration that when mentors operate behind the disguise of a character or false name, that perhaps beginning teachers see that it is permissible to do the same and 'act' within their role rather than 'be' their role. The element of authenticity in mentoring as well as teaching is therefore impacted upon which has the potential also for children to begin experiencing in inauthentic teacher and inauthentic educational settings.

Is the engagement on Facebook destabilising the profession?

This level of authenticity or inauthenticity then leads us to question how stable the early childhood profession is when both mentors and mentees perhaps engage in subjective performances of roles that are not necessarily true to their Being nor true to the profession. As earlier mentioned, beginning teachers are particularly vulnerable in their first years in the workforce which can account for a large number of leavers in the profession due to burnout, dissatisfaction and disillusionment (Macfarlane & Noble, 2005; O'Neill & Stephenson, 2012). Engagement on Facebook is contradictory in this state as it both promotes the early childhood profession through advocacy and support on a much larger scale than small local groups, but also demotes the profession due to the publication of possibly unprofessional dialogue between members as well as inauthentic mentor profiles. One could suggest then perhaps the profession is unstable at this point in its appearance on Facebook rather than destabled. Early childhood has a strong presence on Facebook and an active engagement, which hints to the public that practitioners are committed and motivated to be active in their role as an early childhood educator, rather than disengaged or disinterested. The detachment of Being that Facebook brings however, warns us that whilst educators are active and interested, our behaviour as seen by others must demonstrate professionalism in all spaces, online and offline, which can be exhausting for the educator.

5.2 What impact is it really having?

The impact on the mentor

The impact that comments can have may be profound, not just in practice, but in the professional identity of the educator and in this case the beginning early childhood teacher and their mentor. Should comments be reckless and without the natural filtering of our professional self, then mentoring becomes obscured and uncertainties arise. In addition, when mentors make these reckless comments they may also do themselves a disservice should they wish to become a mentor outside of the virtual world; their profile has already been made public. We then must consider that perhaps the mentors on Facebook also need mentoring in being a good mentor, both online and offline. As discussed earlier good mentoring takes the shape of regular engagement, respectful relationships and reciprocity. In addition to this, whilst mentoring did not actively exist at a formal level when this study began, it now does, albeit new for both the mentor and the mentee, but also in terms of a formal process relating to industrial policies such as teacher registration. This means that further work needs to be done in preparing the mentor for good and effective mentorship when supporting beginning teachers in all spaces of engagement.

The impact on the mentee

The mentee also experiences impact from their engagement on Facebook which can be both positive and negative. On the one hand, they have instant access to a range of ideas, thoughts and solutions to their everyday challenges. On the other hand, this instant access can impede upon their own ability to come up with their own solutions and ideas based upon the theory and practice they have just recently learnt from their undergraduate degree. In addition, beginning teachers are also impacted upon from the modelling of mentors on Facebook which can be both professional and unprofessional, authentic and inauthentic. It is therefore important for the beginning teacher to be taught how to apply a filtering lens to their engagement on Facebook when they graduate and perhaps during their pre-service courses. Universities may need to further explore their content in professional studies and leadership units to have a more significant engagement and analysis of SNSs such as Facebook, Twitter, Pinterest, Instagram and perhaps even Snapchat which is becoming increasingly popular with younger generations of youths. It may even be worthwhile to consider that mentoring programs should include the continued engagement from their trusted and experienced lecturers and advisors as a means of transition to the workplace which include utilising forums on Facebook or designing user-specific forums during the first year of teaching. This is ideal, as academic employees at universities may have access to rigorous courses to further enhance their own skills in mentoring and leadership and therefore provide a more stable environment for the beginning teacher to receive guidance and support through SNSs such as Facebook.

5.3 The next phase of research

In answering the original research question as to whether informal mentoring impacts upon the professional-efficacy of beginning early childhood teachers, we can safely assume from the threads and posts discussed that it does in some way have an effect on educators, both positively and negatively depending upon the nature of the engagement and the vigilance of the administrators of the forums. From here, we take this information and apply it to conversations within the real world as opposed to the virtual world through the tools of semi-structured interviews where participants justify their thoughts and opinions through their actions and verbal words, rather than randomly written pieces of dialogue. They explore what it is to be a good mentor and whether they think this is really happening on Facebook and what impact it is having on them in their daily practice and sense of efficacy as a teacher. Furthermore, a nationwide study reveals just how many of the mentors and mentees believe that Facebook is a positive platform for professional development, efficacy and good mentoring.

References

Badley, G. F. (2015). Qualitative Ranting? *Qualitative Inquiry, 21*(9), 759–765. doi:10.1177/1077800415569791

Crowell, S. (2013). *Normativity and phenomenology in Husserl and Heidegger*. New York: Cambridge University Press.

Ellison, N. B., Gray, R., Lampe, C., & Fiore, A. T. (2014). Social capital and resource requests on Facebook. *New Media & Society, 16*(7), 1104–1121. doi:10.1177/1461444814543998

Fenech, S. (2013). Leadership development during times of reform. *Australasian Journal of Early Childhood, 38*, 89+.

Macfarlane, K., & Noble, K. (2005). Romance or reality? Examining burnout in early childhood teachers. *Australian Journal of Early Childhood, 30*, 53+.

O'Neill, S., & Stephenson, J. (2012). Exploring Australian pre-service teachers sense of efficacy, its sources, and some possible influences. *Teaching and Teacher Education, 28*(4), 535–545. doi:10.1016/j.tate.2012.01.008

Tankersley, A. A. (2010). Discovering curriculum concerns of beginning early childhood teachers. *Childhood Education, 86*, 293+.

Index